skinny ITALIAN

EAT IT AND ENJOY IT

LIVE LA BELLA VITA

AND LOOK GREAT, TOO!

Teresa Giudice

WITH HEATHER MACLEAN

HYPERION

NEW YORK

Library of Congress Cataloging-in-Publication Data

Giudice, Teresa, 1972–

Skinny Italian / Teresa Giudice ; with Heather Maclean.—1st ed.

p. cm.

1. Cookery, Italian. I. Maclean, Heather, 1972– II. Title.

TX723.G58 2010

641.5945—dc22

2009047739

ISBN: 9781401310356

PHOTOGRAPHY BY BEN FINK

BOOK DESIGN BY DEBORAH KERNER

Hyperion books are available for special promotions, premiums, or corporate training. For details contact the HarperCollins Special Markets Department in the New York office at 212-207-7528, fax 212-207-7222, or email spsales@harpercollins.com.

FIRST EDITION

10 9 8 7 6 5 4 3

To *all* my girls . . .
You mean the world to me.

Especially my fabulous daughters

Gia, Gabriella,
Milania, and Audriana

I live for when you say, "You a good mamma!"
I *miei figli sono la mia vita.*

And for my own mommy,

Antonia Gorga,

who taught me to be the woman I am today,
taught me to respect myself, to put family first,
and to always walk a straight line ("like the knife!").
Sei bella in tutti i sensi.
Ti voglio tanto bene Mama, tua figlia Teresa.

Acknowledgments

I would like to thank the following amazing people. I couldn't live without your love and support!

My juicy husband, Joe; my mommy, Antonia; my papa, Giacinto; my brother, Joe, and his family; my mother-in-law, Filomena, and father-in-law, Franco; and everyone else in my wonderful family, here and in Italy and Belgium; my fabulous girls Gia, Gabriella, Milania, and Audriana, for giving me inspiration, making me so happy, and letting mamma make all those phone calls; Heather's husband and her kids Hunter, Hadley, and Gavin for lending me their mommy for a few months; all of my fellow Housewives, especially Dina Manzo and Jacqueline Laurita, for letting me borrow your gorgeous faces and slammin' bodies; Susan Ginsburg, the best agent a girl could ever have, for your vision, dedication, and brilliance; the entire staff at Writers House, the best agency in the world; the amazing group at Hyperion, especially Ellen Archer, Brenda Copeland, Nina Shield, Navorn Johnson, and Shubhani Sarkar for believing in my book and making it look so beautiful; Ben Fink, Jamie Kimm, and Dani Fisher for making my food and my family look delicious; Rick Rodgers, for tirelessly testing the recipes; Andy Cohen and the team at Bravo; my behind-the-scenes production crew friends; Daniel Cerone, my makeup artist; Evelyn Cruz, my hairstylist; my fab friends and colleagues; and finally, my spectacular fans for accepting and loving me even when I flip a table or two!

CONTENTS

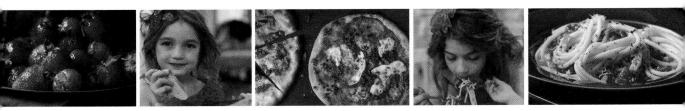

skinny
ITALIAN

1 ❧ Salute!

The first thing people usually say to me when they find out I have four kids is that they could never tell from my body. I thank them, thinking this is a compliment, only to be quickly proven wrong. Follow-up questions immediately include: "What diet plan are you on?," "Do you live in the gym?," and my favorite, "What's the name of your plastic surgeon?"

If you watched the first season of *The Real Housewives of New Jersey*, you know I was brave (or maybe crazy) enough to allow Bravo to film me going through the process of getting my "bubbies" done. If you saw me in the leopard-print bikini, you are totally on my side on this one. I worried, I cried, I kvetched, I kept changing my mind . . . because this was the first surgery I'd ever had in my life.

When in Rome . . .

Salute = sah-LOO-tay

I swear on *Us* magazine, I have never had lipo, a tummy tuck, a "mommy makeover," or even a C-section. All of my children were born the old-fashioned way: with lots of pushing, screaming, cursing, and, thank God, pain medication. I am a big fan of the epidural. Big knives near my body? Not so much.

I must exercise religiously then, right? Our lady of the heavens, no! I have four little ones to chase after; I barely have time for a manicure. We don't have a workout room in our house (unless you count the bedroom, which I do . . .). I don't have a personal trainer or yoga master or whatever. I have no strict exercise regimen, although I'll admit, I like how I feel after I work out. But it's not my thing. I'd rather enjoy life with my kids than live in a gym.

And, let me assure you, I eat. I freakin' love food. Always have. Always will. Food is an integral part of my life and the lives of my family and friends. It's how we communicate, how we love, how we laugh. Food is our second language. It's lovingly prepared, shared, toasted, savored, slathered (you read that right), and occasionally, if you push my buttons, thrown. Food is such a sensual pleasure. The thought of shoving your fingers into freshly made dough, of licking the dripping tomato sauce off the spoon . . . I'm making it sound like a giant aphrodisiac, and as I sit here, looking at the four beautiful kids Joe and I created, I'm thinking maybe it is.

Eating is definitely one of the greatest joys on earth, and I wouldn't give it up for anything. My mother, who never dieted a day in her life, used to shake her head and say, "Think of those poor women on the *Titanic* who refused dessert!"

In other words: life is short; pass the cannoli.

I'll admit, before I was on TV, I never thought so much about my own body and the way I eat. You think you've spent your entire adolescence in front of the mirror, but until you're cornered at Costco with curious fans literally picking through your cart to see what you're buying, you have no idea. It's bizarre. Suddenly, everyone wants the skinny on my ass.

And honestly, I don't blame them (although, if you see me, please keep your hands off my fresh vegetables—that kind of skieves me out). I like to know what my friends eat. I'm interested in Oprah's favorite foods. Actually, I like Gayle's picks better; girlfriend knows how to enjoy her food!

And everything about food and nutrition in this country has become a big confusing mess. Is Splenda safe? Nutrasweet? Olestra? Which one gives you the runs? Seriously, somebody tell me because I am *not* having that.

What's in one day is out the next. Remember when eggs were the enemy? Now, they're fine. For a while, you were supposed to eat lots of meat—was that the Atkins, Pritikin, or caveman diet?—then suddenly, meat wasn't okay. Now, half the "experts" say you need protein at every meal, and half say you don't need it ever. Milk was bad, then it was good, then it was even better because it was supposed to help you lose weight. Now I've heard it's going back on the bad list. Too bad, because my girls drink milk, milk, milk all day long, and there's no chance I'm stopping them. They love it! Me too.

Even the government and all those nutritional experts don't know what's what, since they had to change their little nutrition pyramid guide into some weird triangle thing that nobody understands.

Like you, I have more than one friend who's been on so many different food plans, she's completely forgotten how to eat. Jill pours salt over her food to make herself stop eating. I've actually found Leah picking brownie crust out of her trash can. And Heidi went to a no-carbs boot camp and went so crazy, I had to block her number from my cell phone until she promised to eat a piece of bread.

I'm not a nutritionist or food scientist or a fancy chef. I'm just like you: a regular girl with two eyes and a brain and enough common sense not to buy any of this crap. I've always loved my body, and I've been eating the exact same way since the day I was born. I can tell you in two words why I can eat, eat, eat and still look fabulous: Italian food.

Both of my parents were born and raised in Italy. I was actually conceived there right before my parents moved to America in 1971. (My ma didn't even know she was pregnant. She just wondered why her clothes kept getting tighter.) My brother and I grew up in Paterson, New Jersey, but inside our house, it might as well have been Salerno. We ate real Italian food—not the bastardized fast-food version of it—every single day. My ma shopped at the farmer's market and the local Italian grocery to make sure she could get the same little envelopes of spices and secret ingredients from home. Real Italian food uses olive oil, not heavy cream. We grill and sauté; we don't bread, dunk, and deep-fry. And we use fresh ingredients, not stuff floating in formaldehyde (I know canned foods don't really have formaldehyde in them, but all those preservatives and artificial flavorings are still like poison to your body).

You and I both know gorgeous Italian women who are skinny not because they eat healthy Italian food, but because they starve themselves. But that's the exception, not the rule. You can find neurotic people who obsess about food from any ethnicity. (Bethenny, honey, you really want me to order a steak and only eat three bites of it? Are you freakin' kidding me?)

I'm eighteen months old here with my daddy and mommy. How cute are they?

Need proof that Italian women who cook and eat up a storm of true Italian food can still have fabulous figures? Google Giada De Laurentiis, drool for a minute, and then come back to me.

I want everyone to be able to enjoy *la dolce vita*. I'm going to teach you how to throw painful portion control (and even your measuring cups) out the window, to enjoy, entertain, and eat the most luscious foods on the planet, and to love-love-love your life and the body that comes with it.

Welcome to the Italian way of life. *Salute!*

What exactly do the Italians know about food and health? In a word: everything. We've had more than two thousand years of practice. The oldest surviving cookbook in the world, *De Re Conquinaria*, is from Italy. Apicius is believed to have written it in the first century A.D., and you can bet your ass it doesn't include wheatgrass or tofu.

Italian food was named the favorite cuisine of 72 percent of the 500,000 Americans polled by *Food & Wine* magazine (and you know why). It's easy to forget, however, that it's some of the healthiest food in the world. Our national toast, *salute*, means "to your health." And we mean it. According to

Say My Name

All right, I'm sick of everyone mispronouncing my last name. I've noticed that people from other cultures will talk with perfect American accents until they say their name, and then they sound like they just got off the boat. But not us Italians. We'll let you butcher our names to bits. No more!

To be honest, I didn't actually realize I could do this, just reclaim the correct way to say my name, until my friend's family did. Her maiden name was Zavagno, and everyone said it like this: "Zah-VAG-no." For twenty years, they were the ZaVAGnos, until one day, the youngest son couldn't take it anymore and started making everyone say "Zuh-VON-yo" instead. Within a year, it stuck. It's not a snooty thing; it's a you-want-people-to-say-your-own-damn-name-correctly thing.

So, here we go. My last name is **Giudice**. You've probably heard it pronounced "jew-dice" since I've been on TV, but that's wrong (Andy Cohen at Bravo, I'm looking at you!).

Say "Judy Chay" really fast. Now put the emphasis on the first syllable and slow each syllable down a bit: "JU-dee-Chay." Now add your best Italian accent, and we're good!

Giudice actually means "judge" in Italian, so I believe I have the power to make this change permanent. Court dismissed!

the CIA's World Factbook 2009, for all our fancy technology and advanced medicine and world-class hospitals, the average life expectancy in America for a woman is eighty years. In Italy, it's eighty-three. Imagine adding three entire years to your life! And for eating bread and pasta? Gimme some of that!

Before we get into more of my Italian heritage, I want to get into yours. Italians are famous for their hospitality, and I want you to feel truly at home here, together in our little Italian book. No matter where your family is actually from, considering the Romans conquered pretty much the entire world, it's safe to say that you're Italian too, whether you like it or not. But you will love it, I promise!

I've got a college degree in fashion, not food, but I think growing up in a 100 percent Italian household, speaking the language since I could talk, and eating my ma's cooking since I could walk, more than qualifies me to dish on the deliciousness of Italian cuisine. I make my own sauce (of course!), and also my own sausage, and even wine (not to sell or anything, just to always have what we like on our table). My husband and I opened a traditional Italian restaurant in Hillside, New Jersey: Giuseppe's Homestyle Pizzeria. My dad is there every day, helping plan the daily specials from the Old Country.

My husband and my in-laws are Italian too. My "juicy" husband, Giuseppe (most people call him Joe), was born in Italy. Both Joe's and my parents are from the same small town in Salerno, Sala Consilina, although they didn't become friends until they all moved to America in the 1970s. When he was three years old, Joe was actually in the hospital with his parents the day I was born, waiting to meet me; so I guess he's been chasing me since I came out of the womb.

We had a crush on each other all through our childhoods (yes, we even "played house"), although my mother always warned me against liking him because he was a "bad boy." He was a whole twelve years old at the time.

TOP: Me on my first birthday. Can you imagine letting a baby hold a knife that big? Ah marone!
BOTTOM: Me and my baby brother, Joey. How cute is he?

We've been married for ten years and are blessed with four beautiful children. Food is such a major part of our lives, and I'm so happy I now get to cook in the kitchen with my kids.

When we were growing up, both Joe and I had kitchen chores and had to be at the dinner table cleaned up and on time every night. Things were different back then: the man expected dinner on the table, kids quietly wait-

My wife is a great cook. I don't know how she does it, constantly running around with four munchkins. Where she gets her energy from is beyond me, but Teresa is always hustling.

My favorite meal that Teresa makes is her oven chicken and potatoes. And her steak and vegetable salad. She also has this amazing veal and peppers dish.

But don't be fooled: my wife did not know how to cook when we got married. She learned everything from her mom over the phone. I have to say, she learned pretty quickly, and now she's great at it. She makes up her own recipes and we still have a big family dinner every Sunday at two o'clock.

Trust me on this, Teresa is an amazing woman, but if she learned to cook great home-made Italian food when she was twenty-seven, you can start anytime, too!

---

ing in their seats for him, when he walked in the door. Yeah, I know there are tons of men—Joe included—who would love that to be the rule today, too. But the men used to come home at 5:30 every night. That's right, 5:30. When's the last time you or your man were home for dinner at that time? Joe comes home at a different time every night. I never know when to expect him. How am I supposed to have a hot dinner ready?

I do make dinner for him and my family, of course, five nights a week (Friday is family restaurant night and Saturday is date night), but I generally don't get started until he gets home. The beauty of Italian cooking, though, is that most dishes are so simple, especially if you have certain sauces and herbs around at all times, that they can be made pretty quickly. Fresh, quick, easy, and delicious? Sign me up, right?

I'll cook anywhere. My husband and I go over to Chris and Jacqueline Laurita's house a lot. The men play poker while we cook. Well, let's be honest, I cook and Jacqueline watches. I'm kidding (sort of). She makes appetizers and I'll make the main course. Open a bottle of wine, catch up on all our gossip, it's *the best*!

October 23, 1999—My Shakespeare in Love–themed wedding. Don't you love the poet sleeves on my dress?

Jacqueline is allergic to seafood, which is fine since my husband has a tendency to let all of the crabs we catch at the Jersey Shore go when he's had too much to drink. (There's this little bushel with a top on it that sits in the water to keep the crabs alive and fresh, and what does Joe do? He flings the entire freakin' crate into the ocean so hard, the top falls off, and the whole bucket swims away. He had to make the trip of shame to the grocery store that night for store-bought crabs . . . and gelatos of apology. I'd forgive anyone who brings me Gelotti's, my favorite ice cream shop in Paterson. Well, almost anyone.)

All right, I have a confession to make. It's been ten years since my first solo Italian meal. If you do the math, you'll quickly figure out I haven't been cooking since I was a kid. In fact, I didn't know how to cook at all until I got married. I helped in the kitchen, of course, but I wasn't allowed to touch anything important or mix things or taste and experiment, so mostly, like any kid, I did my chores in a trance. Italian mammas are famous for taking care of their families so well that their kids never want to leave. Most Italian boys go right from their ma's house to their wife's. Same with me and Joe. I was super excited to get married, but once it was all over and I was standing in the kitchen, preparing to make my first "married" meal, I panicked. I had no idea what to do. When you're dating, everything you make for your guy is good. But now I felt like the bar was raised a bit. Like he was going to compare whatever I cooked him to his mom's fabulous food.

I reached for the phone, called my own ma, and cried to her like a baby (in Italian, of course).

It's hard for any woman to match up to the last woman in her man's life, especially if she was a super cook, and especially if she was an Italian mamma. Joe's mom is a great cook, but you understand, I had to be better.

The way I eventually won Joe over was by using some reverse kitchen psychology. Instead of refusing to do things "the way his ma used to do it," I took every chance I got (innocently of course) to use Joe's secondhand recommendations. And almost every time, they led to some kind of explosion.

I would be heating the olive oil and he'd say, "You have to add water to it. That's how my ma did it." I knew this wasn't right (you add water to the tomato sauce later, but not the hot oil), but I wanted him to see it with his own two eyes. I added the water to the saucepan and snap, crackle, pop, we were both covered in hot oil bubbles.

It didn't take too many times of him having to wipe up his wise-ass mess before he realized I was a pretty good cook all by myself.

She actually taught me how to cook over the phone. That should tell you how easy it is to make delicious Italian food. Me, I'm not going to wait until my girls get married to teach them how to cook. I'm starting now, even though they're tiny. They have their little jobs in the kitchen, and I just love to be around them and cook with them.

Since not everyone has a relative from the Amalfi coast to call in a cooking crisis, I decided to write this book to pass on some of our family's tips, tricks, and traditions. It's a love letter to my mamma. It's a lesson plan for my kids. And it's a "welcome to the family" for you. I'm far too young to be your mother, but I'll be your Italian best friend—the fiery, kind of crazy one, who's always good for a bottle of wine, a big dish of pasta, and a million laughs.

Some stereotypes are true: everyone loves an Italian girl. I'll teach you how to embrace your inner *paesan*, how to cook like Mamma, entertain like an angel, and how to stoke the fires in your kitchen, relationships, and even the bedroom.

Allora! Let's get started!

2 ∾ The Cornerstones of Italian Cuisine

(or Things Not Found at the Olive Garden)

I'm sorry if this dashes your dreams, but you gotta know this: the Olive Garden does not serve Italian food. They serve *American*-Italian food; and there's a big, big difference—a difference you will see in your big, big butt if you only eat that kind of food.

Every one of our families came to America from another country at some point in time, and brought with us our cultures, traditions, languages, and, of course, food. But when it's all thrown into that great big "melting pot," sometimes the ingredients get more than a little muddled.

I love-love-love my country, but we're not known for having the healthiest national foods. (God love us, but what other country serves deep-fried butter-on-a-stick?) The Americanization of Italian food has unfortunately given a lot of Italian food a bad rap for being unhealthy.

Ravioli is a perfect example. The Italians have been eating the small envelopes of pasta stuffed with herbs and meats for more than seven hundred years. It's a cheap, easy, and nutritious food supposedly invented by sailors when they stuffed bits of their leftover dinner into balls of pasta to save it for later. Fast-forward to America and the invention of "toasted ravioli"—where a perfect ravioli is prepared, but then dipped in eggs, coated in bread crumbs, and thrown in a deep fryer full of freakin' vegetable oil like common French fries. Now you have 50 percent more calories and more than twice the fat. (I'm sorry, Andy Cohen at Bravo, I know you grew up in St. Louis where toasted ravioli was "invented," I know they even served it at your high school, but it's a big fat fake! It's not Italian food, and p.s., it's not even "toasted"!)

And pizza?

Don't get me started. What began in the Mediterranean as a lovely, rustic flatbread topped with local vegetables, herbs, and eventually tomato sauces morphed in America into a giant, doughy, greasy, cheese-filled monster with entire other meals like cheeseburgers and barbecued chicken thrown on top. I'm not sayin' American (especially Chicago-style) pizza doesn't taste good. But it's a bastardized, belly-bulging version of what the Italians would eat.

Of course *pizza* and *ravioli* and *pasta alfredo* are all Italian words, so it's easy to think they are Italian foods. But, if you're in a typical American store or restaurant, they're probably as authentic Italian as the Dolce & Gabbana handbags sold on the corner of Fifth Avenue.

No one likes a poser. So how can you tell the difference between true Italian cuisine and a knockoff? Here's a handy cheat sheet.

True Italian Food, or How to Spot a Knockoff

REAL ITALIAN	CHEAP IMITATION
Olive oil	Vegetable oil
Butter	Heavy cream
Sautéed	Deep-fried
Pasta is a part of the dish	Pasta is the entire plate
Vegetable-based sauce	Creamy sauce
Lots of vegetables	Starch, cheese, and meat
Fresh Italian cheese	Processed cheese
Sugar in dessert only	Nondessert recipes that call for sugar
Clear salad dressing	Solid salad dressing
Thin, crispy bread	Fat, doughy white bread

It's been estimated that 90 percent of the "Italian" restaurants in the United States are actually American-Italian and don't serve authentic Italian food at all (in my opinion, it's higher than that, but whatever). I can spot those places from the sidewalk. Here's the dead giveaways that you *won't* find in a true Italian restaurant:

- Red-and-white-checkered tablecloths
- Empty bottles of Chianti used as candleholders
- Huge baskets of white bread
- Butter with the bread
- Fake marble heads or other Roman-like ruins made from Styrofoam
- Fake vines painted on the walls
- An indoor fountain

Authentic Italian cooking is healthy because it includes sautéing with olive oil, not deep-frying in vegetable oil. It uses fresh ingredients, including lots of green vegetables. And carbs are a supporting player, not the star of the show.

Just looking at a plate will give you a good idea. An Italian meal will look fresh and healthy. There will be roughly the same amount of vegetables, meat, and pasta. The sauce will be proportionate to the pasta or meat, and it will be part of the meal, not a sloppy afterthought. If you find yourself faced with mountains of pasta drowning in a creamy sauce that is congealing because it's so fatty, with sad, soggy vegetables suffocating under the sauce and grease and oil spilling over the edges of the plate, then you've got yourself a faux and fatty Italian meal.

Another giveaway is the bread. Italian bread is a dainty, savory appetizer, not a bottomless basket of butter-covered bread sticks as big as a baby's arm. The bread world is the opposite of the bedroom world: small is good; big is bad.

When in Rome . . .
bruschetta = bruce-KET-ta

Ignore those giant white loaves you see in the grocery store marked "Italian bread." Not healthy. Authentic Italian bread includes *grissini*, pencil-sized sticks of crispy breads, and *bruschetta*, small slices of bread grilled and then topped with garlic, extra-virgin olive oil, and usually fresh vegetables. (I'll teach you how to make these in Chapter 10!)

Of course, when you cook with me, you're cooking the Old World way. But if you're out, and you're still not sure if you're being served an authentic Italian meal or an American-Italian heart-attack-on-a-plate, see how you feel at the end of your dinner. True Italian food makes you feel full and energetic and satisfied (maybe, if it's good stuff done right, even a little turned on . . .). Italians are hard workers. They eat to fuel up and then go back out into the fields. Faux Italian food makes you feel overly full, bloated, and a little mad at yourself for the indulgence. If you've ever had to secretly undo the top button of your pants under the tablecloth, you know what I'm talking about. No one leaves my house clutching their belly and joking about how much they shouldn't have eaten!

I Heart Healthy Foods

Of course, you should enjoy what you eat, but your body should benefit from it as well. Another reason authentic Italian food is not just good, but also good for you, is that it naturally includes many of the "superfoods" proven to reduce the risk of heart disease, cancer, high cholesterol, and even depression: olive oil, tomatoes, garlic, oregano, basil, parsley, spinach, and fresh fish. In fact, doctors and nutritionists recommend you eat these things every single week. Forget those giant, gaggy supplement pills, and get healthy by cooking the Italian way!

OLIVE OIL

There's so much to say about this amazing oil that I'm setting aside the very next chapter to rave about it. In the meantime, know that olive oil is not only delicious, it also helps your heart, fights cancer, controls your blood sugar, lowers blood pressure, prevents bone loss, stops that little pooch of belly fat from forming (swear!), and can even make you a better lover (well, that last one's not been scientifically proven or anything, but it makes sense that if you're healthier and skinnier then you'd be better in bed, yes?).

From Italy, with Love

Before we can begin dicing, sautéing, and preparing it, let's go over exactly what Italian food is (besides the obvious: the yummiest food on the planet). I'm sure you recognize most of the foods, but I just want to make sure you remember that Italy didn't just bring us spaghetti, but also polenta, prosciutto, and penne. It's easy to forget, when all the foods are grouped together at the grocery store, which ones we can get on our knees and thank Italy for. Here's a quick list.

Italian-Italian Food

Pasta
  (we'll cover this completely in Chapter 6)

Pizza
  (thin crust, rustic)

Ravioli

Lasagna

Salami

Prosciutto

Osso Buco

Pancetta

Minestrone

Ciabatta

Panino

Focaccia

Mozzarella

Provolone

Parmesan

Asiago

Fontina

Mascarpone

Gnocchi

Orzo

Polenta

Risotto

Simple Green Salad

Panzanella Salad

Oil and Vinegar Dressing

Olive Oil

Pesto

Marinara

Biscotti

Gelato

Granita

Panna Cotta

Cannoli

Tiramisù

Zabaglione

San Pellegrino

Chianti

Sambuca

Grappa

Cappuccino

Espresso

American-Italian Food

Calzone
  (just looking at this triple-the-carbs-stuffed-with-cheese beast should tell you it was invented in America!)

Stromboli

Toasted Ravioli

Macaroni and Cheese

Muffaletta

Panini
  (the buttery, gooey, fattening kind)

Frittata

Chicken/Veal Parmesan

Alfredo Sauce

Italian Bread
  (big white loaves)

Caesar Salad

Italian and Creamy Italian Dressing

Pizza, Americanized

Italian Beef Sandwich

Spaghetti with Meatballs

Parmesan Cheese in a Can

TOMATOES

Oprah's smokin'-hot doctor friend, Dr. Mehmet Oz, was one of the first physicians to bring the awesomeness of the tomato to light. In the best-selling book *You: The Owner's Manual*, he and his coauthor, Dr. Michael Roizen,

write that the risk of getting certain kinds of cancer seriously decreases when people eat ten tablespoons or more of tomatoes or tomato paste every week. (This can supposedly cut your risk of breast cancer by 30 to 50 percent! Think pink and eat red!) Tomatoes are full of nutrients and antioxidants like lycopene that are more easily sucked up by the body if the tomato is cooked, and especially if they're eaten with a little olive oil. *Delizioso!*

GARLIC

Did you know that a serving of garlic has more than twenty different nutrients and minerals in it, even calcium, potassium, and vitamin C? Or that garlic was used as an antibiotic before penicillin was invented? Or that if you cook it with parsley (another Italian superfood), it cuts down on garlic breath? (I didn't know those first two either, so don't feel bad.)

Doctors have known for centuries that garlic has many health benefits, but they still aren't sure exactly what makes this smelly little vegetable so good for you. (Is it the selenium? The allicin? The sulphur? Or maybe just magic?) Studies have shown garlic cuts cancer rates, lowers blood pressure, and can possibly even protect the stomach lining (although be careful eating it raw . . . too much can burn your mouth or intestines, especially in little kids).

Garlic Mythology ⚜ ⚜

Most of us have heard about garlic's power to keep vampires away, and many people in Europe used to hang braids of garlic outside their doors for protection. Priests even used to pass garlic out in church to help keep evil spirits away. (Maybe that's what I need to pass out when we're filming *The Real Housewives of New Jersey*! A garlic a day keeps the you-know-what-who-sleeps-with-married-men away?)

OREGANO

Aside from tons of vitamins and nutrients, oregano also has more concentrated antioxidants than blueberries, has antibacterial properties that will help keep your entire system healthy (even protecting you from other germs on other foods), and actually counts as a dietary fiber.

Worried about all the crazy infections that are now resistant to antibiotics, like MRSA? Me too! (I'm healthy, but it's my four girls I worry about. I freakin' hate germs.) Well, here's some good news for Italian-food lovers: in 2008, scientists discovered that the oil from oregano actually kills the MRSA bacteria better than eighteen other antibiotics! Just another reason why home cooking with your own herbs can help your family's health. (Who the hell knows what's in some of that packaged food? Not fresh, infection-kicking oregano oil, I promise you that!)

BASIL

Basil is jam-packed with vitamins and antioxidants, but it also has unique antibacterial qualities. The oil in basil can actually kill bacteria near it and in your body. Adding basil to your recipes (especially things that aren't cooked, like salads) can help protect you from the possibility of getting sick from the germs on other foods. (Kind of makes me want to stick a bottle of basil in my purse to sprinkle over raw foods when I'm in restaurants . . .)

Fiber-licious

We all know you're supposed to eat a fiber-rich diet. And tons of products, even fruity kids' cereals, are now advertising how they're all full of whole grains. So it seems like whole grains are where we should get most of our fiber, right?

I thought so, and so did a lot of my friends, until Caroline Manzo's poor daughter Lauren went on the Cereal Diet. I don't know if you've noticed, but those grains, if you eat too much of them, can scratch the hell out of your insides (and the smell that's released in the process . . . damn!).

Depending on only whole grains for fiber can actually end up hurting your digestive system, as the little seeds can stick in tiny holes in your intestines and stuff.

Looking for a softer, gentler source of fiber? Spinach and dark green salads are great, as well as crunchy vegetables like carrots, celery, and green beans. But the skins of softer veggies and fruits—the apple peel, the potato skin—are also super great. So your grandma was right: the "good stuff" really is in the peel!

PARSLEY

I'm always a little sad when I see parsley sitting on the side of a plate in a restaurant as a garnish. Italian cooks know parsley not only adds great flavor to most dishes, but it also adds amazing health benefits. Can you believe parsley has three times as much vitamin C as an orange, and twice as much iron as spinach? Parsley also helps fight cancer, is full of antioxidants, makes for a healthier heart, and can prevent arthritis. So eat up! (Just don't eat the garnish in restaurants. My friends who were waitresses in college tell me those aren't always washed so well.)

SPINACH

Spinach is another wonder food that Italian cooks use a lot. It's a great source of iron, beta-carotene, vitamins A, C, E, and K, and calcium. Spinach has lots of fiber to help keep your system running smoothly, and doctors believe it also helps fight against cancer, especially lung and breast cancer.

The antioxidants in spinach (there are more than thirteen different kinds) have also been shown to help your body fight stomach, ovarian, prostate, and skin cancer.

Catherine de Médicis, the sixteenth-century queen of France, was actually born in Florence, Italy. Spinach was her favorite vegetable, and she took it with her to France and made the cooks place almost every meal on a bed of spinach. To honor her hometown, she called every dish with spinach *à la florentine*. So next time you see "Florentine" on a menu, you'll know that the dish has lots of healthy spinach and you can toast our great Italian/French queen.

FRESH FISH

Italy is a long, skinny country (even its shape is sexy and skinny!) that touches the sea on more than 85 percent of its borders. That makes more than 4,700 miles of coastline and lots of opportunity to fish. Fresh fish has been a main component of the Italian diet for thousands of years, everything from swordfish to clams to anchovies. Fish has lots of nutrients and protein, but very few calories and fat. Doctors (like our friend Dr. Oz) believe that the oils in fish can not only help your heart, but also make you smarter. Dr. Oz and Dr. Roizen also suggest that fish oil can also reduce your wrinkles, improve your eyesight, and even help with postpartum depression.

Of course, you want to start with the freshest fish possible. At the market, make sure to look the fish in the eye. It should stare back at you. If its eyes are cloudy, it's no good. The fleshy side of the fish should bounce back quickly when you press on it with your finger. And it should never smell fishy. (Really, should anything? I think not.)

A Feast for the Eyes

Authentic Italian food is a lot like an Italian woman: it's beautiful, it has great proportions, it's sexy, vibrant, and colorful, and it smells wonderful. Both Italian food and a good Italian woman will fill the entire house with love.

3
Blessed Virgin: Olive Oil

I love-love-love my skinny jeans. And I know you do too. If I can teach you nothing else in this entire book except the insane importance of olive oil, you will be on your way to a healthier body and to getting in (or staying in) your skin-tight, ass-magic jeans forever. Yes, olive oil is that big of a miracle.

I'm not a doctor, but you can ask any one of them, and they'll tell you about how adding olive oil to your diet helps keep your heart healthy, lowers cholesterol, helps fight cancer, keeps your brain and hormones working, and can help control your weight. Skinny Italian anyone? You need to use olive oil in your diet. Every single freakin' day. If you can do nothing else, at least do this. Even if you can't manage the Mediterranean lifestyle in any other way, even if you can't live without a daily helping of fried chicken and chocolate cupcakes, if you use olive oil whenever possible in your cooking and baking, your body will reap the benefits. (But you do know that no matter what anyone tells you or sells you, if you eat fried chicken and cupcakes every single day, you might as well use your skinny jeans as a scarf . . .)

Growing up, we used olive oil for everything, and I still do. It's so delicious, I don't think I could live without it! Homer (the Greek poet, not the Simpson dad) called it "liquid gold." But supposedly only half of the households in America have a bottle of olive oil in their kitchen. Well, together, we're going to change that, right here, right now. I know it's easy for me to say "just eat olive oil" because I've been eating it my whole life, but I'm also fabulous, and I want you to be fabulous, too. And olive oil, my friend, is one of the keys.

Fear of Fat

The word *fat* has become such a bad word in our culture that no matter what doctors and nutritionists say about adding a small amount (like 2 tablespoons a day) of healthy fat to your diet, I don't think most people do. Fat just seems like the enemy. And it's so confusing to figure out which fats are good and which are bad that it's easier to just try and avoid them all. I get that. I never heard about trans fats when I was a kid, did you? And all of a sudden, everything is "trans fat free." What the hell was it when I was ten, trans-fatastic?

My girlfriend Millie was over for lunch the other day, and I made us some salads. She freaked out when I poured olive oil on my lettuce because I was "eating pure fat." (I used salt and pepper and a little vinegar too, of course.) She's on this crazy weight-loss plan, so she actually had her own salad dressing *in her purse*. It was this calorie-free, fat-free crap. Seriously, it tasted like crap. I told her this, of course, but she said it didn't bother her because it was healthy. How's it healthy? I asked. She said because it didn't have any calories or anything, so it "didn't count."

Here's my question to her: how can something be nothing?

How could she actually be eating *something*—a bright orange liquid pretending to be salad dressing—and claim that it's *nothing*? It's not air. It's something going into her body. And best I can figure, since it's not a recognizable "food," like something you could find in someone's garden, and has no calories, it's nothing but chemicals. Even though it says no calories and no fat, useless chemicals cannot be helping your body.

Even though we'll eat crappy-tasting chemicals we can't even pronounce to try and avoid fat, fat is not a flat-out bad thing. Your body *needs* fat, not just to cushion hard places and drive the boys crazy, but to run properly. Every single cell in your body needs fat to stay together. Your nerves need fat to fire off their little messages. Fat protects your internal organs. And your big, fat brain is 60 percent fat.

You're born with fat, yes, but your whole life, your body needs to keep making new cells to replace old ones, so you need to keep giving it fat. The trick is to give it healthy fats. And olive oil is the healthiest, purest oil on the planet. You can live skinny—yes, you can fit into those skinny jeans!—and still enjoy fat. Trust me on that.

Comparing Cooking Oils: Chemical Cocktail vs. Fruit Juice

Even though they're not all made from vegetables, in cooking, "vegetable oil" generically refers to any oil you can eat or safely cook with that was somehow derived from a plant. So while the label might say "sunflower" or "canola" or "corn," the recipe will just say "vegetable oil" or "cooking oil." All of these oils are processed to the heavens, and don't have any noticeable taste, so you can interchange them in any recipe.

Olive oil is different, though. First of all, olives are a fruit. They are pressed to squeeze out their juices, so olive oil is a fruit juice, or fruit oil, really. If you buy the right stuff (and don't worry, I'll help you), olive oil is nothing but pure juice from the olive. The lack of processing is one of the reasons olive oil is so healthy: it gets to keep all of its healthy components, like antioxidants.

What's a Canola? ⚜ ⚜

Canola oil is often advertised as being as good as, or even healthier than, olive oil, but I'm not buying it (seriously, I'm not buying it). Olive oil is cleanly pressed. Canola oil, like all the other "vegetable" oils, is chemically processed to hell and back.

But my biggest question is: what's a canola? I never heard of a canola vegetable. Turns out that's because there isn't one. It's a freakin' made-up word!

Canola is, no joke, the combination of the words Canada and oil. Great, but what the hell is Canada oil? In the 1960s, looking for a cheap way to grow and process cooking oil, Canadian scientists messed around with the rapeseed plant (which is poisonous to just about every living creature) to try and get it to grow without all its poisonous acids. It worked, sort of, and they got a rapeseed plant with "low acid." They figured out that no one in America would want to buy "rape oil" (even though that's what they call it in Europe), so they decided to make up a name for it.

My friend Jodie didn't believe me when I told her canola wasn't a real plant, so she called the 800 number on a bottle of canola oil that will remain nameless. The customer service agent told her that canola was a pretty yellow flower (that's what rapeseed is). Jodie's feisty like me, and asked why she'd never seen or heard of a canola plant before, and the lady told her that you could "only find them in Canada" because of the "special soil" up there. Hilarious (and untrue; they grow it in America, too).

Here's what I know: the rapeseed plant and the canola plant have the same scientific name, *Brassica napus*. "Canola" is just the nicer new nickname for an unpleasant-sounding plant. Hopefully there's not enough poison in rapeseed/canola anymore to hurt humans, but since it's a new invention, I'm going to wait this one out. I'll stick to the juice from real fruit that's been used for thousands of years, thank you very much.

P.S. In Italian, *cavolo* means "crap." Interesting, no?

The other oils, though, aren't as lucky. Because they don't come from a juicy fruit in the first place, getting oil out of them isn't as easy as simple squeezing. Vegetable oils go through a bunch of processes that include adding chemicals to remove the color, the odor, and the taste. Lots of crazy chemicals. And in that process, the original plant is stripped of almost all of its nutritional goodness.

No matter what health benefits they are claiming on their packaging, no other oil is as pure or as healthy as olive oil. See an oil that's labeled "cholesterol free"? That's nice, but all vegetable oils are cholesterol free. See another oil labeled "light"? They must be referring to the color, because every single oil has the same 120 calories and 14 grams of fat per tablespoon, even olive oil. The big difference is olive oil is pure fruit full of nutrition and healthy fat your body needs, and vegetable oils are unhealthy, chemically treated nonsense.

Good Taste

I've heard many people complain about the strong taste of olive oil. First of all, be serious, olive oil is hardly the least tasty thing you've ever put in your mouth. But I guess compared to other oils it can seem intense, because other oils are processed to hell on purpose so they don't taste like anything. The best olive oil is only squeezed, and only one time, so it does keep some of the olive's original flavor. But that's a good thing!

I get it that something like anchovies is an acquired taste, but you can find an olive oil that suits you right now, no problem, because olive oil isn't just one taste. It's not like a banana that pretty much tastes the same no matter where you get it. Olive oil is more like wine; there are tons of different tastes because there are so many different kinds of olives (more than a thousand varieties), and so many different things that go into making it: the taste of the olive, where the olive is grown, how it's harvested, how it's processed, the time of year, how good the

Teresa's TIP

You can throw out your bottle of vegetable oil (please!), but many packaged foods have vegetable oils hiding in them. To avoid those foods, look for the words hydrogenated or partially hydrogenated on the list of ingredients (the nearer to the top of the list, the more of it there is in the food). You'll be surprised how much stuff—especially kids' food!—is chock-full of bad oils.

I would rather my girls ate a huge bowl of ice cream (a nice, natural one with a few pure ingredients) than a "100-calorie" snack cake stuffed with cream made from the juices of who knows what.

The best way to keep the gunk out of your family's diet is to make as much of the food you eat yourself as you can.

maker is . . . you get the picture. With wine, there are some that you might think are too strong, and some you just love. Same with olive oil. Some taste fruity, some taste buttery, some taste spicy. There are endless options, and there's no excuse for not finding one you like and using it!

While we're talking about taste, just like wines and grapes, the fresher the olive, the better the olive oil. I'll tell you how to find the best olive oil, but if you ever run across some that smells or tastes disgusting, you've got yourself some bad oil. There are lots of ways olive oil can taste, but it should never taste musty, rancid, like wood, like burnt caramel, like dirt, like nail polish remover, like stale milk, and funnily enough, like wine.

Remember, olive oil is used with foods, and not just tossed down like a shot. But the tastes you can expect from good olive oils are grassy, like a vegetable taste; nutty; citrusy like an orange or lemon; floral; spicy; buttery; even bitter is OK—but bitter like a grapefruit, not like a rotten peanut.

A Necessary Expense

I think another reason people aren't using olive oil as much as they should is because of the higher price. A big old bottle of vegetable oil is two dollars, but a smaller bottle of olive oil is anywhere from five to twenty dollars. You have to remember, though, that you use vegetable oil by the cupful in recipes, and you'll usually only use olive oil in tablespoons and teaspoons. A small bottle of olive oil will last you much longer than a bottle of vegetable oil, so it's really not that much more expensive. And I'm pretty sure it's cheaper than a triple bypass, so think of it as an investment in your health.

One way to save money on your olive oil purchases is to buy two different qualities. When you use it as a condiment, you want a really good-quality extra virgin since the olive oil is the most important flavor. But for cooking, you'll be using the olive oil with other strong flavors like meats and vegetables, so you can use a less-expensive extra virgin olive oil. Keep the expensive oil in a fancy bottle on your counter (out of direct sunlight), and put the less-expensive bottle away in the pantry for cooking.

Teresa and I have been to Italy a bunch of times, and of course, there are olive trees everywhere. I know she's telling you that olives are a fruit and all, but believe me when I tell you, you do not want to pluck a fresh olive off the tree and eat it. You will find yourself very embarrassed at having to spit it out in front of your host, tour guide, or loved one. Fresh olives do not taste good. They're disgusting, really.

I know you've had "plain" olives at bars and parties, but they weren't really plain, they'd been cured first. There are a bunch of different ways to get the bitterness out of olives (even soaking them in water will eventually do it), but trust me, your plain olive is really a processed olive.

You can find fresh olives at special markets, but people use those to do their own curing or pressing. Except for those raw-food people, who I hear do try to eat fresh olives. Good luck to 'em!

A Stranger to Olive Oil

It didn't occur to me that some people didn't actually know how to use olive oil until my friend Samantha told me she didn't know what to do with it. Vegetable oil is a no-brainer because we've seen it on TV since we were little. That nice mom from *The Brady Bunch* even did commercials for her favorite vegetable oil. It's the stuff you pour in a pan, or use to bake things. It's the big, sticky yellow bottle at the back of everyone's kitchen cabinet. Olive oil can be used just the same way. Any time you read about, think about, or are told to use teaspoons or tablespoons of "vegetable oil," substitute olive oil instead. If you read about, think about, or are told to use cups and cups of oil, stop right there. Even olive oil will not save you.

Just to be sure you're comfortable, though, I'm gonna walk you through it. There are three main ways to use olive oil in the kitchen: to cook with (you'd better start doing this immediately!), to bake with (not as common, but can easily be done), and to use as a condiment directly on foods like salad and bruschetta (there is no other way!).

How to Cook with Olive Oil

Cooking with olive oil is easy. Anytime you need something in the pan to keep your vegetables or meat from sticking, use a couple tablespoons of olive oil instead of vegetable oil, canola oil, butter, or those cooking sprays. Olive oil is great for sautéing onions, pan-roasting potatoes, and browning chicken, but it will also make your pancakes and eggs taste divine. Instead of soaking your pancakes in vegetable oil and then slopping butter on top, use olive oil from the get-go and you won't even want to use syrup!

One of the reasons olive oil is so yummy for cooking is that when it's heated, it creates this crispy layer on the outside of the food instead of soaking into it. The layer helps the food cook, keeps the juices in the food, and it also adds extra deliciousness. You should always heat up the olive oil in the pan before you add any food (to keep the food from just sucking up the oil), but as long as you don't overheat it to a crazy-high level, all the nutrients and antioxidants and good stuff in the olive oil will stay intact even when you're cooking it.

If you're grilling and don't need a cooking lubricant, you can always brush olive oil onto your food right before you serve it. You'll get an even better taste and all the healthiness you need in just a few-second swipe.

How to Bake with Olive Oil

Olive oil can also be used in your baking recipes instead of vegetable oil. Remember, vegetable oils and canola oils don't have any taste whatsoever because any remnants of flavor from the original ingredient are chemically beaten out of them. I don't notice any difference when I bake with olive oil, but if you're concerned, get an olive oil with the lightest taste. Even if you have to use a blended olive oil, you're still much better off than using plain vegetable oil.

But didn't I just say in the "olive oil is expensive" section that you'll only be using it in little amounts? How can you afford to pour giant cupfuls of it into a brownie mix? You can't, and you really shouldn't; shouldn't be making

recipes that call for giant cups of oil, that is. There are thousands of sinfully delicious recipes that use much less harmful ingredients: chocolate, sugar, cream. Vegetable oil is really, really bad for you. If you find a recipe that calls for lots of oil, look for a different recipe. (You can even make brownies with applesauce instead of oil. I've done that with my kids, and the result was the opposite of the natural food desserts by certain reality cooks that I've tasted at events. Opposite as in, my brownies were really delicious. Opposite as in, didn't taste like dirt.)

How to Eat with Olive Oil

Because it does have a taste of its own, olive oil is great just poured over almost any food, but especially foods with a light flavor. Obviously it's great on salad and bread, but olive oil is also amazing brushed over corn on the cob, sprinkled over veggies, or drizzled on baked potatoes, pasta, or sandwiches.

Fancy Bottles

My daughter Gia asked me the other day why the bottle of olive oil on our counter—the one we use for salads and dipping—has a crooked tube on the top when our ketchup bottle doesn't. Isn't that a great question from my baby doll? It's because we want to have as much control as possible when pouring oil, especially over foods to be eaten immediately. Instead of allowing the oil to come out slowly and then in a big glob, the way ketchup does, the spout keeps the flow consistent. Keeps us from drowning our food, wasting olive oil, and making a big, fat mess.

Looking for the greatest present for your friends or family members? Get a few empty small glass bottles with spout tops at the store, and paint the outsides all pretty to match their kitchens (or have one of your children or nieces or nephews do it). Then get a big bottle of really good extra virgin olive oil, and fill all the smaller bottles using a funnel. Now present it by telling them how much you love them, that you want them to have the healthiest heart possible, and how to use their new best friend: olive oil.

Any time you would think about using butter, use olive oil instead. I know butter is creamy and delicious, but if you can make this simple switch, think of how much more bread and pasta you'll be able to eat and still stay skinny and gorgeous. Go buy yourself a pretty decorated bottle with a pouring spout, fill it with olive oil, and put it on your kitchen table so it will be impossible not to use it.

How to Store Olive Oil

Since it's a fruit oil with very few additives, olive oil won't last forever. Air, heat, and light will break it down, so it's best to keep your olive oil in a dark, cool place, like your pantry. If you must, because you live in a really hot place or something and even your pantry isn't cool, you can store olive oil in the fridge. However, it will get cloudy when it's too cold. Doesn't mean it's spoiled, just means it's cold. Once you bring it back to room temperature, it will clear right up.

If you just have to have a pretty bottle of oil on your kitchen windowsill, get a decorative one with herbs and fruit slices in it and stuff. Just don't open it!

Darker glass bottles are better than lighter ones, and tin cans are great, too. Just don't put olive oil in plastic containers since the oil will suck some of the chemicals out of the plastic. Olive oil should always have a cap on it as well.

Olive oil is best eighteen months after it's bottled. If you have a jar from 2002 in the back of your pantry, it's most likely spoiled and shouldn't be used.

That olive oil doesn't last forever is another reason to take price into consideration. You don't need to use that much, and you can't use it forever. So stay away from the big bulk bottles. They won't save you any money in the end (unless you buy one and split it with your friends, as long as you all have good containers to store it in).

How to Buy Olive Oil

I hope by now I've convinced you that olive oil is your new best friend. You're ready to commit, to go steady with olive oil, to bring it home to meet your ma. You go to the store, proud of your decision and happy with yourself (and happy in general because shopping is the best), and there, in the aisle of olive oils, you're suddenly deflated. Like you spent weeks getting ready for a big event only to have NeNe—freakin' NeNe of all people!—show up wearing the same dress as you.

Why in the hell does shopping for olive oil have to be so confusing and horrible? My guess is because more people are buying olive oil every day to get healthy, and big companies can't stand not to cash in. So instead of just the few simple choices we had a few years ago, now there are hundreds of bottles.

Don't panic. I have a plan.

We'll make sure Sheree "accidentally" leaves NeNe's name off the guest list, and we'll walk through everything you ever needed to know about buying olive oil in a few simple sentences.

Buying Olive Oil: The Skinny

In a hurry and just want the skinny? Buy EXTRA VIRGIN olive oil. Period.

Got more time to look? For your best bottle: get 100 percent Italian olive oil made from 100 percent Italian olives, harvested and pressed at the same place. Look for a nice Italian company (not an American company with a fake Italian name for branding), and make sure it's as far from the expiration date as possible. If you want to save money, for your cooking bottle, get extra virgin olive oil as freshly made as possible, with at least some of the olives from Italy.

Why? Good question. Let's find out.

Olive Oil Making 101

Olive oil was originally made by squeezing olives with big rocks, and then later by pressing them between screened platforms. The olives were squeezed just one time, no heat or chemicals were used, and the oil that came out was the purest and the best. This is called the "first press." Only oil that is removed from the first pressing can be called "extra virgin" or "virgin." This is the only oil we want. If it's not a virgin, keep walking. (Seriously, you boys could learn a few lessons from olive oil.)

Today many companies use fancy centrifugal machines instead of presses to get this first juicing out, but everyone still likes to advertise "first pressing" or "cold first press."

The actual color of olive oil can range from gold to green, depending on the olives. Look for something with a rich color, as a really light hue probably means other stuff was added to it.

Olive oil is usually clear, but it will cloud up when it gets cold (that's

why you shouldn't store it in the refrigerator). If your house gets really cold and you notice your olive oil bottle is cloudy, don't worry, it's not a sign that it's rotten or anything. Just leave it in a warmer place for a few hours, and it should clear back up again.

OO, VOO, EVOO, WTF?

When the very best olives in the crop are picked and pressed within twenty-four hours, you get the very best oil. This we call **extra virgin olive oil** (or if you're a Rachael Ray fan, EVOO). Again, don't even bother with anything else.

Ideally, the story would end here, but not all olives are perfect, and growers don't want to waste the bumped, bruised, or not-quite-ripe ones. So companies use the less perfect olives to make a product of lesser quality: **virgin olive oil**. Same process (although usually not done within twenty-four hours of picking), same chemical-free juice of the olive, just with subpar olives. The price difference between extra virgin and virgin isn't great enough that I would ever buy oil from possibly rotten or picked-up-off-the-ground fruit.

The pressing process leaves behind lots of olive pulp and stuff, so in an effort to make something oily out of even that, companies will add chemicals to the olive leftovers and get themselves some more oil. This we call

The Oil of Old People

If you go to Italy and ask the beautiful locals how they stay so youthful and gorgeous, most of them will tell you "olive oil." Instead of fancy moisturizers or creams, they slather on the olive oil and have dreamy, creamy skin.

Olive oil might just be a fountain of youth, since one of the oldest people in the world claimed olive oil (which she poured over her food and rubbed on her body) and chocolate kept her hot (I love her already!).

Jeanne Calment lived for more than 122 years! She even rode her own bicycle until she was 100, and for her 121st birthday she recorded a hip-hop album called *Time's Mistress*.

(Maybe that should have been the name of Kim Zolciak's record. Although really, she's sort of the opposite of olive-oil young. Am I the only one who freaked out when they heard how she was only like thirty? Do we even believe this?)

just plain or regular **olive oil**. We don't like this kind of olive oil because it's not fresh, it doesn't use the best olives, and it includes all kinds of chemicals, which really defeats the whole healthy purpose.

Don't be fooled by any other labeling: pure, refined, 100 percent this or that. The most important words on the bottle are *extra virgin* or just *virgin*. If you don't see those, move on.

The Million Other Confusing Label Claims

You're only looking for "extra virgin," so you can ignore almost everything else. Most of the extra words that can make shopping for olive oil confusing are just marketing gimmicks. But be careful, because some of them are purposely trying to trick you into picking the wrong oil. Here's what each of those words and phrases mean, in plain old Housewife:

PURE • A pretty useless word that can mean anything. It's supposed to tell you that there are only olives in the bottle, but since they don't have to talk about the chemicals they used to get there, or what shape the olives were in when they used them, "pure" can be ignored.

NATURAL • Of course it's "natural." What's the alternative to using a "natural" olive? Using a fake, plastic one? Ignore this word. It's completely meaningless.

REFINED • While *refined* sounds like it has fancy manners or something, it really means the olive oil has to be produced using chemicals, filters, and heat that could end up putting toxins in your body instead of antioxidants. Refined oil usually has a funky taste and smell, too. No good for cooking. No good for anyone.

BLENDED OLIVE OIL • We only want extra virgin olive oil, not our precious oil blended with who knows what from who knows where. Blended is good for drinks, bad for olive oil.

OLIVE POMACE OIL • Pomace is the mushed-up olive skin and pits left over after pressing. Using the pomace (and lots of chemicals) to create some olive oil is like using the hair caught in your vacuum cleaner to make your own extensions. Nasty. Avoid, avoid, avoid.

LIGHT OLIVE OIL • The same guys who'll try to sell you the Brooklyn Bridge are trying to trick hyper-dieting Americans into buying crappy oil. Since all olive oils have exactly the same amount of calories and fat per serving, there is no such thing as a "light" olive oil in terms of calories or fat. Somebody at some crappy company realized that if they took inferior olive oil (which is lighter in color because it's so crappy) and called it "light," referring to its color, they might trick people into buying this kind of oil. You're far too smart for this con.

FIRST PRESS • Completely unnecessary. If it's extra virgin, it's first press (and most of them aren't even really "pressed" anymore). You can ignore this.

COLD PRESSED • Same as with "first press." Ignore.

Fresco e naturale

ULTRA, PREMIUM, OR ULTRA PREMIUM • These are just show-off words. They don't really mean anything except that the company thinks its olive oil is great. It might be, so you don't have to avoid these words. Just don't let them sway your shopping decision.

TRADITIONAL • I think this label is hilarious because it's not a regulated word; anyone can stick it on anything. I saw it on a bottle that also had "composed of refined olive oils and virgin olive oils" on it. What's traditional about mixing junk in with the good stuff to stretch your profits? N*iente*!

ESTATE GROWN • What estate, where? And are the olives all from the same estate or from a bunch of different estates in skievy places? Meaningless.

UNFILTERED • You can find this on extra virgin olive oil, and basically it just means they didn't strain out every single little piece of olive skin or pulp from the oil. Some people say this makes the tastiest oil. Some people think it makes the oil expire faster. If you don't mind little specks floating in your oil, go for it. Me, you know I'm all about cleansiness.

HANDPICKED • This is supposed to tell you that they treat their olives with TLC, which is fine, but there are also nets and rakes and some machines that are used that do just as good a job getting the best olives off the tree. Handpicked is sweet, but it might mean you're paying more for the oil because their labor costs are higher.

MADE IN ITALY, IMPORTED FROM ITALY, 100 PERCENT ITALIAN • These all sound good, but you have to look at the other writing on the bottle to figure out how good it really is. Ideally, you want an extra virgin olive oil that is made in Italy with only Italian olives from the same property. Most bottles I've seen with "made in Italy" on them go on to tell you that it was also made with olives from Spain, Greece, Turkey, and Italy. Why is this bad? First of all, I'm biased, but Italian olives are the best. And since olives are tastiest when they are handled carefully and pressed within twenty-four hours, the thought of a bunch of ragtag olives being shipped

in from different countries on boats and trucks and stuff doesn't really appeal to me.

The Very Best for My BFFs

We're clear that extra virgin olive oil with 100 percent Italian everything is the best way to go. You'll still have a dozen different choices, though.

Looking for the premium pick to impress your in-laws, your frenemy, or that freakin' guy from the IRS that won't stop knocking on your door even though you explained to him a million times that pretending to make giant purchases in cash was just a joke for your TV show? Like wine, the best stuff comes from small companies that grow, harvest, press, and bottle their olive oil all at the same place. These are usually family companies with a long history and reputation to protect. Try a few to see which one you like best and enjoy!

No More Bottled Salad Dressing . . . Ever!

Now that you're all olive oil savvy, it's time to take the solemn oath of Italian eating. Repeat after me:

> *I promise that I will never, ever again, as long as I live or expect to be friends with Teresa, purchase creamy, crappy, fatty, chemical-filled, already-mixed salad dressing. I will instead save money, love my heart, worship my body, and live like an Italian by making my own, which will in turn impress my friends, make my neighbors jealous, and make me that much sexier to the love in my life.*

I'm so proud of you! Of course, you need a kick-ass, homemade, authentic Italian salad dressing recipe now. And I just happen to have the perfect one.

Sexy Italian Salad Dressing

Olive oil

Balsamic vinegar

Parmigiano-Reggiano cheese

You're looking for measurements, right? Now's when you're going to have to jump in and be a hands-on Italian cook with me. For most things, we just eyeball the ingredients, adding more and less of what we like.

Here's how I make my salads: I get the lettuce all ready in a big bowl (and add cranberries or whatever else I want in it), then I get my bottle of olive oil and just pour it over the top (probably for 2 seconds). Next, I pour balsamic vinegar over the top (about 1 second of pour). Then, instead of using salt, I sprinkle Parmigiano-Reggiano cheese over the top. (Some people also use black pepper, but my dad can't eat it, so I never use black pepper in anything.)

Now stick your fingers in and mix the salad up with your (clean, washed) hands. Massage the oils and cheese all throughout the salad so you get the flavor in every bite. Sexy and delicious! (Now go wash your hands again.)

4 ∽ Italian Seasonings

What's What and Who's Who

In college, there are certain classes you have to take that you know are gonna kill you. If you're a communications major, you dread the science requirements. If you're a football player, math is probably not your thing. So to save their students' GPAs, most universities have beginner classes specially designed for the nonexpert. Even though the class might just be listed as Geology 101 in the course catalog, the students know the awesome nicknames that tell it like it really is: Rocks for Jocks, Physics for Poets, and my favorite, Math for Plants.

I didn't go to culinary school and I'm assuming you didn't either. But since we're probably not going to go now, and we've got a mess of Italian food to whip up, we need a beginner course on the spices, herbs, and special flavors used in Mediterranean cooking.

Herb or Spice? ❦ ❦ ❦

How do you know if something is an herb or a spice? Scientifically there is a difference (but barely, and those science guys are still arguing about it): herbs are supposed to come from the leafy part of the plant, and spices from the seeds, fruit, bark, or roots.

The better question is: should you say the *h* in *herb* like they do in London, or use the *h*-less *erb* like they do in Paris? *Herb* comes from the Latin word *herba*, which means "grass," but I asked around, and basically, in America, you can say it however you want.

In New Jersey, at least my friends and I, we vote for Paris. I say *erb*. Jacqueline says *erb*. My friend Edel says *erb*. Caroline had my favorite answer, though. She tells me that in Brooklyn, where she was born, it's *hoib*.

Love it!

Teresa's T·I·P

Using a salad spinner is a fast, easy way to gently wash and dry fresh herbs.

Welcome to Vines for Virgins.

So that you never again just grab the bottle called "Italian spices" and shake it over your chicken, I'm going to teach you what these wonderful ingredients are for, how they taste, how to cook with them, and even how to store them.

At the end of each section, as a reward for being a good student, I'm going to give you one of my delicious and juicy recipes that star the herb you just learned about.

Basil — BASILICO

Looks like: Green leaves, kind of like peppermint.

Tastes like: Spicy sweet, with a bit of anise (licorice-like) flavor.

Dry or fresh: Dry basil doesn't have any taste, so only use fresh. (Those bottles of dried basil in the grocery store are a joke. You might as well crumble dead leaves from your doorstep over your food.) Good fresh basil leaves are healthy-looking and dark green. Don't use one with dark or yellow spots.

Where to get it: Grow it yourself, or buy it fresh at the market. It's usually only available fresh in the summer months, but you can easily freeze it to thaw whenever you need it.

How to prep it: Wash leaves gently since they can bruise easily. You can use both the leaves and the soft stems. You can slice, chop, mix in a food processor, or just pop whole leaves or a whole sprig into your dish.

How to eat it: You can eat fresh basil raw or cooked in just about anything. Whole leaves and soft stems are also edible.

How to cook with it: Too much cooking will break down basil's flavor, so you should add basil at the end of the cooking process.

How to store it:

Fresh • Do not put fresh basil in the fridge unless you like black, slimy things. Instead, treat fresh basil (from your garden or the grocery store) like you would cut flowers: trim the end, and stand them upright in a jar of water. If you keep them out of direct sunlight and change the water every day, fresh basil can last like this for weeks! (Keep it in there even longer, and eventually it will sprout roots and you can plant it in your garden.)

Frozen • There are two methods for freezing basil: leaving it whole, and chopping it into ice-cube trays. To freeze it whole, you first have to blanch the plant, which means dipping sprigs in boiling water for fifteen seconds, and then in ice-cold water (this toughens the skin to survive the freezing process, otherwise it will turn black again). Dry the leaves well on paper towels, line them up on a plate or pan, and put them in your freezer. Once they are frozen, take them out and wrap them in paper towels, put the bundle in a

Teresa's TIP

Another fun way to use frozen basil ice cubes is to just remove them from the freezer and then use a cheese grater. Grate right over your prepared dishes, and the basil will defrost instantly and you'll get a great taste as well as a great puff of aroma!

plastic freezer bag, and remove as much as you need throughout the year. To use ice-cube trays, finely chop the basil leaves on a cutting board or use your food processor with a little olive oil drizzled in. Put 2 teaspoons of the chopped basil in each ice-cube space, and add water. Once the cubes are frozen, you can pop them out and put them in plastic freezer bags for easier storage. To use the cubes in recipes, either let them thaw in a strainer (to drain off the water), or pop them right into your soups and sauces.

Dried • I just told you not to use dried, so don't.

Best in: Pesto, tomato pairings (add to tomato soup—yum!), with olive oil, in sauces, over meats. Joe even eats big, fresh basil leaves on his burgers instead of lettuce. Phenomenal!

Fun fact: In ancient times, the Greeks and Romans thought that to get basil to grow well, you had to curse like a maniac while you were planting it (I think I'd be a great basil farmer! "Grow, you prostitution whore! Grow!!!"). In French, the way to say someone is raving, like foaming at the mouth with all their b.s., is *semer le basilic*, which literally means they are "sowing basil."

T-Sizzle's Basil-Lemon Drizzle

MAKES ABOUT
6 TABLESPOONS,
4 SERVINGS

This is a great way to try your hand at using basil. This drizzle is really versatile. I usually make this to serve over grilled chicken breasts, but you can also try it over vegetables, steak, pork chops . . . just about anything but dessert.

½ **garlic clove**

1 **cup packed fresh basil leaves**

¼ **cup fresh lemon juice**

2 **tablespoons extra virgin olive oil**

¼ **teaspoon salt**

⅛ **teaspoon freshly ground black pepper**

1. Fit a food processor with the metal chopping blade. With the machine running, drop the garlic through the tube to mince it.

2. Stop the machine and add the basil. Pulse a few times to chop it. With the machine running, add the lemon juice, oil, and 2 tablespoons water and process into a thin sauce. Season with the salt and pepper. Let stand at room temperature until ready to serve, but no longer than an hour.

Capers ❧ CAPPERI

Looks like: Small green bud about the size of a kernel of corn, kind of like shriveled peas.

Tastes like: Tangy, lemony, salty.

Dry or fresh: Actually, neither. You get capers in a jar already pickled. They are the unbloomed flower buds of a prickly Mediterranean bush that are picked, dried, and then cured in salt or vinegar. You'll have two choices: capers in salt or in brine. Capers in salt look drier and have big sea-salt crystals on them. Capers floating in brine (that weird colored liquid) lose some of their flavor and texture because of the brine.

Where to get it: You can find small jars of capers in the grocery store, usually by the jarred pickles and olives. You can also get them at an Italian market or online.

How to prep it: If you're using capers stored in salt, soak them in water for 15 minutes and then rinse before using to get rid of all that salt. If you're using capers in brine, some people rinse them once before using, but I think that gets rid of too much of the flavor.

How to eat it: You can eat them right out of the jar, or put them straight into your recipes. They don't have to be cooked, so they can be tossed onto salads.

How to cook with it: Just add capers whole to the recipe as they're required. No smashing or cutting needed.

How to store it: Once the jar is opened, you'll need to store them in the fridge. They'll last six months or more in there, though, as long as they stay covered in brine.

Best in: Sauces, salads, veal or chicken piccata, or served with smoked salmon or grilled swordfish.

Fun fact: Capers are thought to help reduce flatulence. (I always add some to my Italian bean soup, just in case.)

SEXY SWORDFISH
WITH CAPERS AND LEMON

MAKES 6 SERVINGS

What makes swordfish sexy? I don't know. It just is. My family loves fish, and we eat it all the time. This is one of our favorites.

2 garlic cloves, crushed under a knife and peeled

2 tablespoons extra virgin olive oil

One 2 1/4-pound swordfish steak, about 1 3/4 inches thick, cut into 6 portions

1/2 teaspoon salt

1/4 teaspoon freshly ground black pepper

1/4 cup fresh lemon juice

3 tablespoons drained capers

1 tablespoon chopped fresh parsley

1 teaspoon dried oregano

1. Heat the garlic and oil together in a large skillet over medium-high heat until the oil is hot and the garlic is lightly browned and very fragrant, about 2 minutes. Remove and discard the garlic.

2. Season the swordfish with the salt and pepper. Add to the skillet and cook until the underside is lightly browned, about 3 minutes. Turn and brown the other side, about 3 minutes more.

3. Pour the lemon juice and 2 tablespoons water over the swordfish. Sprinkle the capers, parsley, and oregano over the fish. Cover and reduce the heat to medium-low. Cook until the fish is just opaque when pierced with the tip of a sharp knife, about 5 minutes more.

4. Transfer the fish to dinner plates. Top with the pan juices and serve hot.

Garlic ～ AGLIO

Looks like: A small, lumpier onion. This is because, unlike an onion, garlic actually has several different sections inside called cloves. Depending on the size, there can be anywhere from ten to twenty cloves in one bulb of garlic. You have to peel and smash your way down to the cloves, but recipes will tell you how many cloves to use. You can store the extras.

Tastes like: It's hard to describe because garlic is garlicky. I guess you could say it's really pungent with a little kick?

Dry or fresh: You can get it fresh, dried, jarred, or powdered, but since you can keep it in a dark cabinet for a real long time, there's no reason not to always use fresh.

Where to get it: Any grocery store, in the produce section. Look for a solid bulb that isn't discolored and is really firm. While the stalk part can be soft, the bottom and sides of the bulb shouldn't be soft at all. You want hard, hard, hard.

How to prep it: Smash the entire bulb (with the palm of your hand or the side of a big kitchen knife) to release the individual sections. Now take each section and smash it again, and the peel will slide right off. Throw away the peel, and you have your clove. You can cut the clove a few times and throw it in your dish, or you can chop it up really fine in your food processor (the fancy word for this is *mince*). In sauces and stuff when you want the garlic flavor really smoothed out over everything, you can use a garlic press. It's a little handheld tool that looks like a nutcracker mixed with a strainer. You put cloves in one side, squeeze, and the garlic spurts out like a juicy paste.

How to eat it: You can eat it raw (sparingly), but most people cook it with their food or put it in dressings and sauces.

How to cook with it: Don't burn your garlic, or it will turn bitter. To keep this from happening, add olive oil and garlic to your pan at the same time, and heat them up together. As soon as the garlic browns, remove it.

How to store it: A bulb of garlic can last several months if it's kept in a dark place with plenty of air circulation. I keep mine in a cabinet under the sink. You can put garlic in a basket, or in a mesh bag, but not a plastic bag and not in the refrigerator because it will get moist and moldy. Once you've broken the bulbs to remove a clove or two, you can put the rest of the bulb back into storage, but it won't last as long. And if you've minced garlic and have some left over, you can store that in the refrigerator in an airtight container for a few days.

Best in: Sauces, seafood, and sausages, although some garlic fanatics put it in just about everything.

Fun fact: If you chew fresh parsley after eating garlic, it's supposed to help take away the garlic smell. I find it's just easier to make sure everyone around you (especially anybody you're going to be kissing later) eats garlic with you. Then all your smells cancel each other out.

Teresa's TIP

Want to remove the garlic smell off your hands after cooking? Rub them around the surface of your stainless-steel sink for thirty seconds. Don't have a stainless-steel sink? You can use the faucet or even a travel coffee mug. They even sell little bars of stainless steel the size of soap for this very reason for about ten dollars. Why does it work? The same reason that your hands smell like metal when you touch a bunch of pennies, only the opposite.

GORGEOUS GARLIC SHRIMP

MAKES 4 SERVINGS

If you're a serious garlic lover (like I am), feel free to add more garlic to the recipe. I usually serve this with rice and steamed asparagus with a fresh lemon squeezed over the veggie.

3 tablespoons extra virgin olive oil

3 garlic cloves, finely chopped

1 ½ pounds large (21 to 25 count) shrimp, peeled and deveined

⅛ teaspoon salt

⅛ teaspoon freshly ground black pepper

3 tablespoons fresh lemon juice

2 tablespoons chopped fresh parsley

1. Heat the oil and garlic together in a large skillet over medium-high heat, stirring occasionally, until the oil is hot and the garlic is softened, about 1 ½ minutes. Add the shrimp and season with the salt and pepper. Cook, stirring often, until the shrimp turns opaque, about 4 minutes.

2. Add the lemon juice and parsley and stir well. Serve hot.

Oregano   ORIGANO

Looks like: Green stalks with small leaves, kind of like mint. It also has pretty purple flowers when it blooms. Dried oregano looks like little flakes of green and brown.

Tastes like: Aromatic, a little bitter, and kind of warm tasting. Really good oregano eaten plain will make your tongue a bit numb.

Dry or fresh: Unlike basil, oregano actually has stronger flavors when it's dried, and doesn't lose its goodness. I usually go for fresh things, but with oregano, I only used dried. It's cheap and easy, it tastes great, it's good for you, and you'll use less of it in your recipes than fresh oregano, so it saves you money.

Where to get it: Any grocery store, in the jarred spices section. It's a classic pizza condiment, so you'll probably see it in little round jars in nicer pizzerias.

How to prep it: No need. Just scoop, pour, or shake it directly out of the jar.

How to eat it: You can use it in recipes, or sprinkle it right into salads or dipping sauces or over pizza.

How to cook with it: Only the leaves are used for cooking. Just measure out how much you need, and add it directly to the dish. It won't dissolve like salt, but will stick to the food.

How to store it: Store the jar in a dark place, like your cabinet. It will last from six months to forever. It will never go bad, but it will lose its flavor eventually.

Best in: Tomato sauces, on pizza, over veggies and grilled meat. It also works really well in spicy food. Oregano goes perfectly with a tomato, any way, anytime, anywhere! When you're using tomatoes, you should automatically think "oregano."

Fun fact: Oregano became popular in America after World War Two when soldiers who had been stationed in Italy brought the "pizza herb" home with them.

Teresa's T·I·P

Many dried spices are also available in a "ground" form that looks like colored powder. Don't fall for it. Unless you're baking, you don't need it. Besides, ground spices lose their flavors the fastest, and cooking recipes are written for fresh herbs, which can be easily converted to dried herbs. Cooking with ground means you'll probably get way too much flavor (and hardly any oils).

TEMPTING TOMATO AND OREGANO CHICKEN SOUP

This soup is nice with Parmesan on top. You can also add rice or tiny pasta to thicken it up—great for cold days.

1 tablespoon extra virgin olive oil

Two 10-ounce chicken breast halves, with skin and bone

1 small onion, chopped

2 medium carrots, cut into ½-inch dice

3 garlic cloves, minced

One 48-ounce can reduced-sodium chicken broth

One 28-ounce can Italian plum tomatoes,
   with their juices, chopped

1 teaspoon dried oregano

¼ teaspoon dried thyme

¼ teaspoon dried sage

½ teaspoon salt

¼ teaspoon freshly ground black pepper

6 ounces green beans, cut into ½-inch dice (1½ cups)

1 tablespoon chopped fresh parsley

1. Heat the oil in a large saucepan over medium heat. Add the chicken, skin side down, and cook until golden brown, about 5 minutes. Transfer to a plate.

2. Pour off all but 1 tablespoon of the fat from the saucepan. Add the onion and carrots and cook until softened, about 5 minutes. Add the garlic and stir until fragrant, about 1 minute. Add the chicken broth, tomatoes and their juices, oregano, thyme, sage, salt, and pepper, and bring to a simmer over high heat. Reduce the heat to low and simmer to blend the flavors, about 30 minutes.

continues on page 59

3. Return the chicken to the saucepan. Simmer for 10 minutes. Add the green beans and cook until the chicken and green beans are tender, about 15 minutes more.

4. Remove the chicken from the soup and transfer to a chopping board. Cool until easy to handle, then cut the meat from the bones, discarding the skin and bones. Cut the meat into bite-sized pieces and return to the pot. Sprinkle the soup with the parsley and serve hot.

• • •

Parsley ⌇ PREZZEMOLO

Looks like: Bright green, tiny, curly leaves; Italian parsley leaves are longer and flatter.

Tastes like: It has a very mild flavor, a bit grassy. Italian parsley has more flavor, but you can use either one.

Dry or fresh: Fresh, if you can. Dried is OK in a pinch, but it's not as flavorful.

Where to get it: You can usually get it year-round at the grocery store. Look for bright green parsley without any wilting edges. Dried parsley will be with the jarred spices.

How to prep it: Wash. Dry. Chop or tear. The end.

How to eat it: You can eat the leaves and the smaller thin stalks. Eat as much fresh parsley as you can, because it doesn't have a big taste, and it's so healthy for you! Throw it on sandwiches and in salads. Add it to your sauces. You can munch on it raw, like celery, especially after you've eaten garlic.

How to cook with it: Parsley needs to be added to your cooking at the very last minute, because heat will break down its flavors quickly.

How to store it:

Fresh • Like basil, snip the ends and place the stalks in a jar of water. For some reason, parsley likes to have a plastic bag over its head, so drape one

Dried Herbs Gone Bad

While some dried herbs can last years in your cabinet, there are a few ways to quickly tell if they are past their prime.

Color =
If the colors are all dull and faded, the flavor probably is, too.

Smell =
If the aroma from the jar is barely noticeable, the taste probably is, too.

loosely over the top of the plant. Change the water every few days, and it will last for up to two weeks.

Frozen • Since most recipes only call for a sprig or two of parsley, many people buy it in a fresh bundle and freeze it, so they always have some "fresh" on hand. Unlike basil (with its bigger leaves), parsley is super easy to freeze. You can actually just freeze it whole. Wash it, chop it up a bit, and let it air dry. Then place it in a plastic freezer bag. Remove what you need, whenever you need it. It will generally thaw right away in your recipes (after being frozen, it won't look pretty enough for a garnish, but it will taste great in your cooking).

Dried • A jar of dried parsley can be stored in a dark cabinet for one to three years.

Best in: Sauces, chicken, eggplant, fish, veggies, pasta, even rice.

Fun fact: In Roman times, it was believed parsley could ward off drunkenness. Possibly a good tip for college girls—arm yourselves with parsley!

SIN-FREE LINGUINE WITH PARSLEY SAUCE

MAKES 6 SERVINGS

You won't believe there's no cream in here! The sauce also tastes great over grilled chicken or fish.

- **2 medium red-skinned potatoes (about 12 ounces), peeled**
- **1 pound linguine**
- **3 tablespoons chopped fresh parsley**
- **1 tablespoon chopped fresh basil**
- **1/2 teaspoon salt**
- **1/4 teaspoon freshly ground black pepper**

1. Put the potatoes in a medium saucepan and add enough cold salted water to cover. Cover the pot and bring to a boil over high heat. Reduce the heat to medium-low and set the lid ajar. Simmer until the potatoes are tender, about 25 minutes.

2. Meanwhile, bring a large pot of salted water to a boil over high heat. Add the linguine and cook according to the package instructions until al dente. Time the pasta so it is done a few minutes after the potatoes are tender.

3. Drain the potatoes, reserving about 1/2 cup of the potato cooking water. Return the potatoes to the saucepan. Using a potato masher or a handheld electric mixer, mash the potatoes until smooth, adding enough of the potato water to make a thick, creamy sauce. Stir in the parsley, basil, salt, and pepper. Cover to keep warm.

4. Drain the pasta, reserving about 1/2 cup of the pasta cooking water. Return to the pot and add the potato sauce. Mix, adding enough of the pasta water to lightly thin the sauce as desired. Serve hot.

Rosemary ⟍ ROSMARINO

Looks like: Prickly blue-green, evergreen needles.

Tastes like: A little like pine, very fragrant.

Dry or fresh: Fresh is so much better than dry (and easier on your mouth and insides), and since you can so easily buy, grow, or freeze it, you should really try and use fresh. If you must use dried, though, I won't blame you. (Although if you cook with full, dry needles, I would try to strain it from the dish before you serve it so your guests don't get a splinter in the roof of the mouth. Not pretty.)

Where to get it: Grow it on your windowsill! It's almost impossible to kill. It's also at the grocery store, in the fresh produce section (look for branches and needles that bend, that aren't dried and dead).

How to prep it: Wash the whole sprig with the water on full force to get the dirt out from everywhere. If you want to just use the needles, hold the sprig at the top with one hand, and run the pinched fingers of your other hand down the stem opposite the direction the needles are growing. They should pop right off, and then you can pull the top needles off by hand. Chop it up by putting the needles in a pile and rocking a large kitchen knife over the pile.

How to eat it: Rosemary doesn't have to be cooked. You can eat the needles chopped up and tossed over a salad or something. But don't eat the stem. In general, you should not eat any stem that's woody.

How to cook with it: If you're using fresh, you can throw a whole sprig (the stem with the needles attached) in what you're cooking, and then remove the sprig before you serve it. If you want to leave the rosemary in the dish, chop it up as small as you like and add it to your recipe. Rosemary sprigs are also great for baking in the oven tied to roasts or stuffed into chicken.

How to store it:

Fresh • In the refrigerator, in a plastic bag for up to a week. Wash right before using.

Rosemary's Bathing

I know I freaked you out with the story of Natalie Wood's downtown champagne burns, but I did remember a bath with food that is safe, sexy, and completely delicious: the rosemary bath.

Here's how you do it:

¼ cup dried rosemary

¼ cup dried sage

2 tablespoons dry oatmeal

Pour all the ingredients into a little satchel or square of cheesecloth and tie closed with a long ribbon.

When you want to use it, tie the bag over the bathtub faucet so the warm water hits the bag before it hits the tub. Your rosemary bath mix will make the water softer and will smell amazing.

Frozen • Wash the rosemary and dry it thoroughly. Then stick the whole branches in a plastic bag in the freezer. Once it's fully frozen, take the bag out and shake the needles off (they come off the stem when it's frozen much easier than when it's fresh; they just fall off). Toss the stem, and put all the needles back in the freezer bag. I actually use rosemary so much that I freeze huge bunches of it, and then store all the needles in a little glass jar in the freezer. Any time I need rosemary, I just scoop it out of the jar, put the jar back, and I'm good to go.

Dried • In a glass jar, dried rosemary will last several months to several years.

Best in: Sautés, stews, stuffings, dressings, and marinades, also with chicken, lamb, pork, and seafood; great with potatoes, and even in desserts.

Fun fact: Rosemary is called the "herb of remembrance," and was used in both weddings and funerals as a sign of love. Brides used to give rosemary to their grooms to ensure their fidelity. Apparently, if the groom couldn't smell the rosemary, he wasn't capable of being faithful. Ladies, get out your herbs!

ROSEMARY POTATOES

MAKES 6 SERVINGS

So quick and easy—especially with the microwave shortcut. We make this at least once a week.

6 small red-skinned potatoes, scrubbed but unpeeled

2 tablespoons extra virgin olive oil

1 teaspoon chopped fresh rosemary
   or ½ teaspoon crumbled dried rosemary

¼ teaspoon salt

⅛ teaspoon freshly ground black pepper

1. Pierce each potato a couple of times with a fork. Place in a single layer in a microwave-safe baking dish and cover with plastic wrap. Microwave on High until the potatoes are about half-tender, about 5 minutes. Carefully remove the plastic wrap (watch out for the steam!), and let the potatoes cool until easy to handle. Cut the potatoes lengthwise into quarters.

2. Heat the oil and rosemary in a large skillet over medium-high heat until the oil is hot. Add the potatoes. Cook, stirring occasionally, until crispy and golden brown, about 8 minutes. Season with the salt and pepper and serve hot.

• • •

Sage ✦ SALVIA

Looks like: Oval, flat, fuzzy, silver-green leaves.

Tastes like: It has a very strong, musty, peppery taste. Use it sparingly, or it will take over the whole dish.

Dry or fresh: Dried sage is another herb that is actually more potent and flavorful than when it's fresh. For that reason (and because then I don't have to use as much, it's easier, and it still tastes great), I use dried sage.

Where to get it: At the grocery store in the produce section, or with the jarred spices.

How to prep it: Wash and pull the leaves off. Cut and go! Or just shake from the jar.

How to eat it: It can be eaten raw, but I'm not sure why you would. It's best used in recipes mixed with other flavors.

How to cook with it: Be careful how much you add since it's a powerful flavor. Cooking over long periods of time does diminish the flavor, so keep that in mind (if you want more flavor, add sage at the end of cooking; if you want it milder, add it in the beginning).

How to store it:

Fresh • Wash and dry and store in a plastic bag in the fridge (although it will only last about four days).

Frozen • Like parsley, you can just stick the leaves in a freezer bag and use them as you need them.

Dried • They'll last in dried form for six months or more in a dark cabinet.

Best in: Fatty meats (because sage is supposed to help digest fat) and to even out really strong flavors, like game. Also great in stuffing, ravioli, eggplant, fish, chicken, and roasts.

Fun fact: Centuries ago, when things were much less clean and hygienic than today, everyone smelled really bad. Especially when a plague came to town or something. Women used to pick little bouquets of fragrant herbs and flowers to hold over their noses when they went out in public—not just to stop the smells, but also hopefully to stop them from catching any germs. The little bouquets were called "nosegays," because in the Middle Ages, *gay* was a word that meant "an ornament" or "pretty" (it still kind of means "pretty," doesn't it?) and the bouquets made things nicer for the nose. A typical nosegay included herbs with strong smells, such as sage, rosemary, thyme, and lavender.

PORK CHOPS ALLA SALVIA

In Italian cooking, we almost always cook our pork on the bone. It gives you much better flavor.

1 tablespoon extra virgin olive oil

Four 8-ounce center-cut pork loin chops, on the bone

1/2 teaspoon salt

1 teaspoon dried sage

1/4 teaspoon freshly ground black pepper

1 cup "The Quickie" Tomato Sauce (page 117)

1. Heat the oil in a large skillet over medium-high heat. Sprinkle the pork with the salt, 1/2 teaspoon of the sage, and the pepper and rub in the seasonings. Add to the skillet and cook, turning once, until browned on both sides, about 5 minutes.

2. Add the tomato sauce and remaining 1/2 teaspoon sage and bring to a simmer. Reduce the heat to medium-low and cover. Simmer until the pork is opaque when pierced at the bone with the tip of a knife, about 15 minutes. Serve hot, with the sauce.

Thyme ⌒⌐ **TIMO**

Looks like: Small green leaves on thin stalks.

Tastes like: Lemony, slightly minty, and peppery.

Dry or fresh: You can use thyme either way: dried or fresh. Fresh has a more subtle, green flavor (and, like rosemary, is super easy to buy, grow, and freeze), but dried thyme holds its flavor really, really well. If you have space and time issues in your kitchen, I'd go with dried. (Unless I were cooking fish, then the green thyme leaves look so much prettier on the dish.)

Where to get it: From the produce section of your grocery store. Or grow it up there on your windowsill, right next to your rosemary.

How to prep it: Wash it. Hold a sprig at the top with one hand and run the pinched fingers of your other hand down the stem. The leaves will fall off.

How to eat it: You can use the leaves directly on salads or in any of your cooking.

How to cook with it: Thyme actually releases its flavors slowly, so it's an herb to add at the beginning of the cooking process.

How to store it:

Fresh • In the refrigerator, but it will only last a couple of days. Wash before you use it.

Frozen • Very similar to rosemary; in fact, I have my little jar of thyme right next to the rosemary in my freezer. Wash the thyme and dry it thoroughly. Then stick the whole branches in a plastic bag in the freezer. Once it's fully frozen, take the bag out and shake the leaves off (they fall off the stem much easier when it's frozen). Throw the stem away, and put all the leaves back in the freezer bag; or do a bunch at once, and put all the leaves in a glass jar in your freezer.

Dried • In a glass jar, dried thyme will last several months to several years.

Best in: Sauces, dressing, stuffing, salads, meat dishes, and seafood.

We're very friendly people, and we like to invite even people we just met over for meals. Teresa and I had only known Danielle for a couple of weeks when she asked if she could bring her kids to our Shore house for the weekend. Of course, we said yes. Teresa and me and our kids were there, and Danielle's new boyfriend, Steve, came as well. I love to entertain. I'll open my house to anyone. But you gotta have respect.

Early Saturday morning, while mine and Danielle's kids were watching cartoons, Steve was in a recliner chair watching with 'em (big kid). Danielle comes in, lies on top of Steve, and starts to go at it right in front of the kids!

I was furious. I grabbed Steve, took him outside, and told him if he ever did something like that again in front of my kids, I'd rip out his tongue and throw it in the lagoon. He apologized and said it was all Danielle, but in any case, respect your hosts. Don't dirty up their house or their kids, or you probably won't find yourself invited back . . . anywhere!

Fun fact: Thyme was thought to give courage, so women often presented a sprig of thyme to knights going off to battle. It was also placed under pillows to ward off nightmares. (I might have to try that tonight. I'm still trying to get the images of Danielle screwing up my Shore house out of my mind. Literally, she screwed the place up . . . in front of my kids, no less.)

CHICKEN BREASTS WITH LEMONY THYME MARINADE

MAKES 4 SERVINGS

This is Gabriella's favorite dinner. It's very light and sweet, just like her!

1/4 cup extra virgin olive oil

2 tablespoons fresh lemon juice

1 garlic clove, minced

1 teaspoon chopped fresh thyme or 1/2 teaspoon dried thyme

1/2 teaspoon salt

1/4 teaspoon crushed hot red pepper

Four 9-ounce chicken breast halves with bones, skin removed

1. Whisk the oil, lemon juice, garlic, thyme, salt, and hot pepper in a glass or earthenware shallow baking dish until combined. Add the chicken and turn to coat with the marinade. Refrigerate, turning the chicken occasionally, for at least 1 hour and up to 2 hours. (Or let stand at room temperature for no longer than 1 hour.)

2. Position an oiled broiler rack about 8 inches from the source of the heat and preheat the broiler.

3. Remove the chicken from the marinade, reserving the marinade. Place the chicken on the rack, skinned side down. Broil for 10 minutes. Turn the chicken over and baste with the reserved marinade. Broil until an instant-read thermometer inserted in the thickest part of the chicken reads 170°F, about 10 minutes longer. Transfer to a platter and serve hot.

Herb Study Guide

You've got all the spice-girl knowledge you need now. But I couldn't leave you without a little study guide. Here's a pretty little chart to remind you which herbs you should get fresh, freeze, grow yourself, or buy in a bottle, and when to add them to your dish.

HERB/SPICE	HOW TO USE IT / WHERE TO KEEP IT	WHEN TO ADD IT TO COOKING
BASIL	FRESH / FREEZER	END OF COOKING
CAPERS	JAR FROM STORE / PANTRY	ANY TIME
GARLIC	FRESH / UNDER YOUR COUNTER	ANY TIME
OREGANO	DRIED FROM STORE / PANTRY	ANY TIME
PARSLEY	FRESH / FREEZER	AT THE VERY LAST MINUTE
ROSEMARY	GROW IT / FRESH / FREEZER	BEGINNING OF COOKING
SAGE	DRIED FROM STORE / PANTRY	BEGINNING FOR LESS FLAVOR; END OF COOKING FOR MORE FLAVOR
THYME	GROW IT / FRESH / FREEZER	BEGINNING OF COOKING

5 ⌒ Fresco e Naturale ❧

Aside from my one, publicly televised bubbie enhancement (and please, we've already been through this; it was very necessary), I'm a natural kind of girl. I like to look good for my husband and for myself, but I'm not out there getting injections, and fat lips, and pimping fake diet pills and stuff. (Hello, O.C. Housewives! Love you!)

If you look past the lip gloss, I'm a simple, honest, straightforward girl. I tell it like it is (obviously). I'm sweet, but I'm also feisty. (And I still got no freakin' skeletons in my freakin' closet. Thank you. Thank you very much!) I'm the same way with my food. I like it simple, I like it authentic, and sometimes, I like it spicy.

Italians take a very simple, natural approach to cooking and eating. It's about enjoying your life, enjoying your friends, eating good food, and drinking good wine. We work hard, and we play hard. I want to teach you how to add healthy habits so deeply into your lifestyle that you don't even have to think about it.

This is not a diet. Diets suck. I don't want you to ever again sign up for a strict, no-fun, no-taste, no-swallowing diet. That approach—that food is the enemy and you must control your food demons—is crap. It might work if we were robots or something, and to get energy we plugged into a nutrient machine, but we're not. We're humans with this incredible body, and everything we need to keep it running right in front of us. Food is our friend. It's one of the greatest gifts we have: being able to refuel our bodies with delicious tastes and textures that can be enjoyed socially, romantically, and always sensually.

A happy, healthy, delicious, sexy life is a great thing to wake up to every day. I want you to love food, love eating, and still love your body afterward. And all three are totally possible if you follow these Six Rules for Loving Your Food and Having It Love You Back.

Rule 1 • No Obsessing

The key to a healthy relationship with food is to stop obsessing about it. It's hard, I know, when we've been obsessing about what we put in our mouths since junior high. (Some of us more than others.) But stop. Just stop. Take a step back, take a deep breath, and take an honest look at how you look at food.

Is food a happy part of your life? Something you look forward to and feel good about afterward? Or do you have a love-hate relationship with it—you love to eat it, but hate all the worry and guilt and self-doubt that comes after? Do you consciously enjoy your food, or is it a chore that must be tracked and accounted for, like pennies in your checkbook?

Obsessing about anything isn't healthy. Not for you, and certainly not for those around you. You're a role model, even if you don't know it. You're a role model to your kids, to your nieces, to your goddaughter, to your friends, to the younger girls on the subway that look to you for what they will or should be doing in their future.

You're sending the wrong message if you're picking out the middle of a bagel and throwing away the outside because it has too many calories.

You're sending the wrong message if you go out to dinner with your friend and eat two bites of his meal, but don't order anything for yourself but a drink because you don't want to get fat. (And you sure as hell won't be invited to dinner with me!)

You're smart. You're strong. You're fabulous. Stop obsessing about food right now. I promise, you can love your food and eat it, too.

Rule 2 • Surround Yourself with Good Friends and Good Food

I know a lot of people who are in abusive relationships with food. They crave, they sneak, they binge, they starve. Some of them even forgot how to freakin' eat healthy, let alone cook!

Remember: food is your friend. If food makes you feel bad, you're eating the wrong food. Get rid of all the processed, unhealthy crap in your house. Don't buy it anymore. Surround yourself with good food so that it's not only a part of your lifestyle, but a part of your environment. Get a pretty bowl, put it out on your counter where you can see it, and fill it with fruit. Have grissini and olive oil on hand in case you get the munchies. You might have to shop more to keep more fresh food around, but it's worth it. You're worth it.

You also have to hang around other people with healthy views on food and healthy eating habits. If your friends make you feel bad about what you're eating, get new friends. Bad behavior is contagious. You'll have a hard time living a healthy, happy lifestyle if you're always surrounded by other people who drink, snort, smoke, or pick at their dinner.

Rule 3 • No Starving Allowed

Your body needs food like a car needs gas. You wouldn't buy your dream car and then drive it on fumes, would you? You'd wreck the engine. You have your dream body right now. It might be covered up by a couple extra layers,

Avoid Stripper Food

but starving yourself will not reveal its better self. It will instead screw up your metabolism, make you miserable, drain you of energy, and scramble your brain.

You are kidding yourself if you think you can starve yourself thin and keep it up. You might get thin, but you'll be chained to the whole no-eating thing your entire life. Once you try to eat real food instead of rice cakes again, your body will freak out, and you'll gain more weight than ever. It's far better to eat a good meal and get a little activity going than to not eat, and not have the energy to walk to the mailbox.

Rule 4 • Eat Real Food

It sounds obvious, but more and more of the "diet," "natural," and "light" foods barely resemble food at all. What's "natural" about a baked "snack stick" in a box? What the hell is a Pringle, let alone a fat-free one? It looks nothing like a potato. Same goes for a "smart puff," a "soy crisp," and a "cakester." Shouldn't food look like . . . food?

We've become used to things like Pirate's Booty and pita chips, but imagine if some guy walked out of the jungle who had never eaten anything but plants, animals, and foods made from just that his whole life. Do you think he would touch sugary cereals or diet sodas? You might as well hand him wood chips and battery acid.

The bulk of your diet should be real food—food from the earth. If your great-grandma couldn't find it in her garden, her farm, or at the grocery, it's probably not good for you.

Another way to know if you're eating a healthy diet of real food: you don't have a baggie full of vitamins in your purse. If you've restricted what you eat so much that you have to swallow your nutrients in a squishy pill, I say that's a problem. You can get everything you need to be healthy (and satisfied!) from real food.

Rule 5 • The Fewer Ingredients, the Better

It's that simple: the fewer ingredients something has, the better it is for you. Number of ingredients in a juicy peach? One. Number of ingredients in an energy bar? I counted more than twenty, including not-so-delicious-sounding things like "organic date paste" and "soy lecithin." (Do not Google that last ingredient. You will not be happy. Oh, and avoid looking up "gelatin." I was sick all night from that mistake!) I don't think I cook an entire meal that uses more than twenty ingredients!

Even in recipes, look for simple and few ingredients. That's one of the things that's so great about authentic Italian recipes: most are made with fewer than seven delicious, nutritious ingredients. If you see a recipe asking for huge amounts of butter or heavy cream, look for another recipe. Or make a variation of your own using extra virgin olive oil. Experiment. Get your hands in there. Food is sensual. Enjoy it!

Rule 6 • Get in Touch with Your Food

You can always look at the ingredients on processed food (and if you can't pronounce it, put it back), but you really don't need to read a word to know if something is healthy or not. You have your five amazing senses, perfectly designed for a job like finding healthy food. Use them!

Look at it. Listen to it. Smell it. Taste it. And, most importantly, touch it. Touch it before you buy it, and after you buy it.

If you can't touch your food before you buy it, you probably don't want it. I'm not saying you have to stick your head behind the deli counter, but you can feel if the chicken is firm or frozen through the wrapper. (Meat in a box? No thank you.) You can squeeze the potatoes in their sack.

Once you get your healthy food home—and wash it, wash it, wash it— enjoy the entire experience of it. You know I toss salad with my bare hands,

Salute!

but I also rub spices into food, push my fingers deep into the dough, and caress my vegetables. Cooking and eating should not be a thing you do without thinking. You should savor every bit of it. Slowly. It's almost like a prayer, the way I cook in my kitchen. I inhale the smells, close my eyes, and I'm thankful. I can't just chop a tomato. I have to love on it first. I might rub it on my cheek or give it a little kiss. So smooth and soft and ripe and juicy. I want to know every corner, edge, surface, and texture of my food. Slowing down and appreciating the entire process will make a huge difference in how you enjoy food, how much you eat, and how your body responds to it.

Where to Find Your Food

By now, you have a pretty good idea of what great, healthy, authentic Italian food is. Before we can cook it, though, we have to find it. Yes, you can find bits and pieces in your local grocery store, but to really get the best, you gotta find a farmer's market.

Farmer's Market

A farmer's market can be an outdoor gathering of different food under different tents, a large indoor market like the one on Route 46 near my house, or even a roadside stand. The important part of the farmer's market is that it offers fresh food grown locally.

Fresh food is important because the longer food sits around, the more chance it has of losing nutrients, going bad, or just not tasting good anymore. The farther food has to travel from where it was harvested, the less fresh it will be when you get it. Farmer's markets sell produce from near your house, so it's got the best chance of being fresh, and you know exactly where it's coming from.

I don't mind bottled or dried food like olive oil or wine or pasta from another country (in fact, I like that stuff the best from Italy), but there is no way fresh food should travel across international borders to get to my table. You have no idea how long it was sitting in the bottom of some boat, how long it was sitting in that country and in our country getting checked in; and other countries do not have the same standards for food that we do. I just heard that more fresh garlic in United States supermarkets comes from China than California now. China? Last I checked, that was pretty freakin' far away from me. I know garlic lasts a while, but I want it to last from the time I get it, not be on its way out as soon as it arrives. And after the pet food and toothpaste and lead paint business, I'm not sure what the heck they spray on their vegetables over there. (If you're not sure where the garlic in your grocery store comes from, look at the roots. American-grown garlic has the roots still attached, but they chop them off to ship them from China. Hairy garlic is good. Bald garlic, bad.)

When you buy from your local farmer's market, you not only know where your food comes from, but you're also supporting people and jobs in your area. The prices are great at farmer's markets, because they don't have to pay for storage at big, fancy stores. And the vendors there are not only nice, they really know their stuff. Make friends with them, and they'll not only help you pick the right food and tell you how to prep it, but they might even save the good stuff for you.

Farmer's markets won't have everything fresh all year long, because not everything grows all year long. That's why you buy it when it's in season, enjoy it fresh, but also freeze it, can it, and preserve it (all of which I'll show you how to do).

Grow Your Own Garden

There's no easier, cheaper, or safer way to get fresh food into your house than to grow it in your own backyard (or rooftop or balcony). During World War Two, people were encouraged to plant "victory gardens" to keep America from having the same food shortages that they had in Europe. More than twenty million American families planted their own gardens and raised 40 percent of the vegetables eaten during those years.

We had a big garden growing up with eggplant, romaine lettuce, tomatoes, cucumbers, zucchini, basil, and parsley. My brother, Joey, and I had to work in it, but it was always really rewarding. You pull a few weeds, you water things, and then you get to pick delicious vegetables and herbs right off the vine or stalk.

Today, they call home gardens "kitchen gardens," and I think everyone should have at least one vegetable or herb they grow themselves. It makes you care about your food that much more because you're actually tending to the plant from when it's a tiny baby. Even the White House finally replanted a kitchen garden in March 2009, for the first time in sixty-six years, after 100,000 people signed a Web site and Facebook petition. (Start yours now! Don't make me have to petition you!)

Unless you live in a part of the United States that has really extreme weather, like on top of a mountain or something, these plants will grow really easily almost anywhere:

- Spinach
- Tomatoes
- Sweet peppers
- Zucchini
- Peas
- Carrots
- Cucumbers

- Green beans
- Lettuce
- Parsley
- Basil
- Thyme
- Garlic

You can start them from seeds, clippings, or sprouts. Check with your local nursery for the specifics on how to best plant in your time zone, climate, and type of soil.

Grow Your Own Right Up There on Your Windowsill

I don't care if you live in an apartment or a mansion, you can grow a couple of pots of herbs in your kitchen. You'll have fresh ingredients right there. You'll have a healthier house because the plants release oxygen. And if you're bored, you'll have something to talk to.

Here are the three easiest herbs to grow inside. They aren't very big, and they are practically impossible to kill. Grow them in individual pots, or get a nice long rectangular planter and have a real kitchen garden.

BASIL

Basil really needs only four things to survive (and keep you in tasty eats all year): high-quality potting soil to start with, plenty of light (artificial light will work), water, and occasionally, some organic fertilizer (but only use half of whatever the bottle recommends). To give yourself a head start, get a basil plant from your local nursery that already looks healthy and pretty. Put it in a pot that has nice drainage, keep the soil moist but not soggy, and you are good to go!

ROSEMARY

Rosemary needs pretty much the same thing as basil: a pot with good drainage, high-quality soil (with some sand in it), lots of light, and occasionally, organic fertilizer (use only half the amount recommended). To tell if you have enough water, push your finger in the soil an inch. If it's dry down there, water it. Rosemary grows really slowly, so pick a plant the size you want it to pretty much stay for several months. Once a year, to give your rosemary plant a little kick, either spread a tablespoon of dried crushed eggshells around the base of the plant, or pour a teaspoon of lime in the same place. You'll know you're doing it right if the needles on your rosemary bush stay bendy.

THYME

Thyme is probably the easiest herb to grow indoors because it needs the least attention. It doesn't need to be watered very often—just once or twice a week—and it will grow in a sunny location all by itself.

Teresa's
T·I·P

Instead of adding salt to most of my dishes, I add cheese instead. Feta, Parmigiano-Reggiano, or mozzarella will give you all the salty flavor you need (without the extra sodium you don't).

Naked Food

I cook for my family almost every night, so I'm not a strict raw foodie or anything, but if you love raw food, Italian is the way to go. Not only are the ingredients we typically use in Italian food fresh and natural and healthy, but a lot of wonderful dishes can be made without cooking at all. I like to call this "naked food"; it doesn't need much more than a chop, some mixing, and you bring the natural flavors together without heat or processing or anything else getting in the way of the food. Here are three of my favorite naked dishes.

Zucchini "Spaghetti" Salad

MAKES 4 SERVINGS

This is a great, fresh side dish, or you can make it a full meal by adding beans, pine nuts, or cheese to the top. I don't peel the zucchini before slicing them because they look so much prettier with their skins on. The twirling bit in step 3 is optional; the longer you let the strips marinate, the more willing they will be to twist. This is a super-easy recipe as long as you have a good slicer (I find a V-slicer, a plastic mandoline with metal blades, works the best).

3 large zucchini (about 1 1/3 pounds), scrubbed well,
   ends trimmed

1 tablespoon fresh lemon juice

1 tablespoon extra virgin olive oil

1/2 teaspoon salt

1/8 teaspoon freshly ground black pepper

1/4 cup chopped fresh basil

1. Using a mandoline, plastic V-slicer, or spiral slicer (or, if you have mad skills, a knife), cut the zucchini into long, thin julienne strips. Do not use the seedy center of the zucchini, as it can be too soft and will ruin the look and texture of the strips.

2. Whisk the lemon juice, oil, salt, and pepper in a large bowl. Add the zucchini and basil and toss well. Let stand at room temperature for a few minutes so the zucchini can soak up the dressing and soften slightly.

3. Using a fork with long tines, twirl each portion of zucchini onto the fork so it looks like a little bird's nest, and transfer to a plate.

Sautéed Zucchini "Spaghetti" with Pine Nuts

MAKES 4 SERVINGS

While we're talking about zucchini spaghetti, I wanted to give you one more way to prepare it. It does use olive oil and heat, but this preparation gives the zucchini a softer texture and slightly different flavor. It's still a delicious vegetarian meal that even the pickiest eater will love.

Eat it naked style, or use your imagination to whip up any number of dishes: add salsa cruda or pesto to the top, sprinkle with cheese, anything is good! Just don't drown the zucchini in too much sauce because you don't want to lose its fresh flavor.

2 tablespoons pine nuts

**3 large zucchini (about 1 $^1/_3$ pounds),
  scrubbed well, ends trimmed**

1 tablespoon extra virgin olive oil

1 garlic clove, minced

$^1/_4$ teaspoon salt

$^1/_4$ teaspoon freshly ground black pepper

1. Heat a large skillet over medium heat. Add the pine nuts and cook, stirring often, until toasted, about 2 minutes. Transfer to a plate and set aside.

2. Using a mandoline, plastic V-slicer, or spiral slicer (or, if you are a skilled cutter, a knife), cut the zucchini into long, thin julienne strips. Do not use the seedy center of the zucchini, as it can be too soft and will ruin the look and texture of the strips.

3. Heat the oil and garlic together in the skillet over medium heat, stirring occasionally, until the garlic is tender, about 1 $^1/_2$ minutes. Increase the heat to high. Add the zucchini and cook, stirring occasionally, just until it is heated through and still al dente, about 1 minute. Don't overcook the zucchini, or it will get mushy. Remove from the heat and stir in the pine nuts, salt, and pepper. Serve hot.

SALSA CRUDA

This "raw sauce" is the Italian version of salsa. Great for dipping crunchy or salty things. Also great over angel hair pasta (cooked, but warm or cold), breads, in salads, just about anywhere!

3 large ripe tomatoes, seeded and cut
   into $1/2$-inch dice

$1/3$ cup chopped fresh parsley

$1/3$ cup chopped fresh basil

$1/4$ cup extra virgin olive oil

1 garlic clove, minced

$1/2$ teaspoon salt

$1/4$ teaspoon freshly ground black pepper

About $1/3$ cup freshly grated Parmigiano-Reggiano

1. Using your hands, combine the tomatoes, parsley, basil, oil, garlic, salt, and pepper in a large bowl. Don't squash the tomatoes, but make sure they get good and coated. Let stand at room temperature for at least 30 minutes and up to 3 hours to develop the flavors.

2. Serve the salsa as desired, and sprinkle each serving with about 2 teaspoons Parmigiano-Reggiano.

6 ❧ And God Said, "Let There Be Pasta."

And There Was • And It Was Good

Famous Italian filmmaker Federico Fellini—whom I adore for giving us both the film L*a dolce vita* and the word *paparazzi*—said, "Life is a combination of magic and pasta." Spaghetti, macaroni, noodles . . . whatever you call it, it's heaven on a plate.

Admit it, you love pasta so bad you can't stand it. You love it in all of its six hundred different forms. I never met a single person who didn't love pasta.

Pasta is an amazing food not just because it tastes great and grabs onto delicious sauces, but also because it's easy to cook, it stores forever, it's cheap to buy, it fills you up, and, as my husband, Joe, says, "With two pounds of pasta, you can feed, like, a generation."

The Truest Truth About Carbs

Unfortunately, much like my beautiful home state of New Jersey, pasta has gotten an unfair rap. Maybe it started with the Atkins guy, but somehow pasta got turned into the boogeyman of bad food—the biggest no-no if you wanted to lose weight or be healthy. Thankfully that no-carbs crap is over. Doctors kept telling everyone you need carbs for your body to function, athletes have always eaten carbs, but I think once the general population realized that without carbs, they didn't have the energy to even get out of bed, they decided carbs weren't so bad after all.

Hear me clearly: carbohydrates are absolutely necessary. They are the main source of energy for our body, our nervous system, and our brain. If you don't give them to your body, you will have to burn fat for energy, which is not good for your figure and can cause nausea, lightheadedness, headaches, weakness, and (ew!) bad breath.

The trick is to eat the right amount of the right kind of carbs. Simple carbs like sugar are absorbed too quickly into the body, give you a high, and then leave you like a gold digger leaves her dying fiancé to party at the river. Complex carbohydrates are digested more slowly, don't screw up your blood sugar, and give you the energy you need.

So we're all agreed, we need carbs. But how many? Before I say another word, for the love of all that is holy, please check with your doctor to see what your daily calorie goal should be based on your age, gender, height, medical history, and all that. (And P.S.—If you blindly follow somebody's 500-calorie-a-day meal plan and go blind, lose your hair, or worse, I will be so brokenhearted. But remember, I told you so.)

To maintain a healthy weight or lose weight, nutritionists agree that you should get only about 55 percent of your total daily calories from carbs. One gram of carbs equals 4 calories, so if you eat an average of 1,600 calories a day, that would be 220 grams of carbs a day. If you eat 1,200 calories a day, you could have 165 grams of carbs.

To put this in perspective, one full cup of pasta is 42 grams of carbs. Crazy, isn't it? I bet you thought a plate of spaghetti was like 1,000 grams of

This one time Teresa and I were making a lasagna from scratch for company, and to hurry things up, we decided to stick the eggs in the microwave. Don't ever do that.

First of all, we forgot we had eggs in there. So when they started exploding really loudly, we couldn't figure out what was going on. It sounded like gunfire or something! We were ducking, our guests were hiding . . . it was crazy.

When we realized it was the eggs in the microwave, *ah marone*, what a mess we had on our hands! There was egg everywhere!

Maybe that's what put Teresa off from cooking pasta from scratch. Our lasagna nearly gave us a heart attack!

carbs, right? My friends and I did too until we crunched the numbers (we're smart chicks here in Jersey) and discovered we really could love our pasta and eat it, too! (Even if you eat more than a cup, relax. If you ate the *entire* box of spaghetti all by yourself, you're still only eating 1,680 calories and 420 grams of carbs. Not healthy, of course, but not knocking-on-death's-door crazy like some of those starvation diets out there.)

So, we've established that a normal serving of pasta doesn't have too many carbs. Let's kick the crap out of some of those other pasta myths so we can start digging in!

Pasta Myth 1 • White Pasta Is Bad

White pasta is often lumped in with white bread, white flour, and white sugar as a "bad" carb because they digest too quickly in your body. But what the hell is "white pasta"? Any pasta that isn't dirt brown or green? Um, that only leaves the yellow or tan pasta.

Maybe the people who warn against "white pasta" are looking at egg noodles or noodles made with processed flour, but Italian pasta is made with a hard wheat called durum that's coarsely ground down to a flour called semolina. (It's so hard, the Italians used to knead the dough with their bare feet . . . no lie!) So Italian pasta is slow-digesting, healthy, and can even be called a whole grain. Ha!

Just make sure your pasta says "100 percent durum wheat semolina" or "100 percent durum wheat." In fact, it's against the law in Italy to make pasta with anything but durum wheat, so if your pasta is imported from Italy, you're good. Most Italian pastas made in America also use durum semolina, so you're probably fine no matter what you pick.

Pasta Myth 2 • Pasta Is Fattening

This one is funny because if you've ever looked at the nutritional information on a box of pasta, it usually says 1 gram of fat per serving. That sounds pretty good to me! It's not the pasta itself that's fattening, it's the crazy stuff people put on top of it (like ten pounds of processed cheese). But since we're cooking the Old World Italian way, we're using our pasta to help dress up fresh ingredients, healthy oils, and vegetables. I know my kids wouldn't just chomp on raw spinach, but toss it in a pasta dish, and they gobble it up.

Pasta Myth 3 • Pasta Has No Nutritional Value

Again, that amazing durum wheat used in Italian pasta making tells a different story. A cup of cooked Italian pasta imported from Italy has 8 grams of protein, 10 percent of your recommended daily amount of iron, and almost the same amount of dietary fiber as a slice of whole-wheat bread. While the Italian government doesn't allow durum flour to be "enriched," some American companies add even more vitamins and minerals, including calcium, potassium, and folic acid, to the protein-and-fiber goodness of semolina flour.

A Pasta Primer

You now have divine permission to eat and enjoy pasta. Amen! The first thing you need to know is that in Italy, they don't call it "pasta." In Italian,

Is It Bad to Munch on Raw, Dried Spaghetti?

It's one of those things you think only you do (or did as a kid) but ask around, everyone at one time or another munched on some raw spaghetti out of the box, usually out of complete boredom.

My grandmother used to say my brother and I shouldn't do it or we'd "get worms." We didn't believe her, but I did wonder if it was bad for your body in any way.

Several doctors I spoke with confirmed that unless there were weevils in your pasta, you had pretty much no chance of getting worms. They did say, however, that pasta is sharp and can cut up your insides, and that since pasta expands in water, it probably wasn't a good idea to go throwing it down your pie hole before cooking it.

My dentist, though, had a very strong opinion: she said to cut it out right now. Like chewing ice, biting down on dried pasta can damage your teeth in a million ways. My dentist also won't allow me to give my kids those fruity snacks, and they've never had a single cavity, so I guess I'm going to listen to her, and try to find something new to chew on.

pasta means "paste," and ordering a plate of paste just doesn't sound so good. In Italy, they say *macaroni*. It's sort of like opposite world: while in America "macaroni" only refers to the short elbow-shaped (or sometimes SpongeBob–shaped) noodles in a box with an envelope of cheese powder stuff or a fatty, homemade casserole oozing with cheese, in Italy, you can order macaroni and expect a sophisticated, lovely meal.

I also want to clear up the different types of pasta. There are really only two: fresh and dried. Pasta isn't like bread, where there are a million different recipes and tastes depending on what loaf you buy. Pretty much all pasta is made from the same ingredients: flour, water, salt, and sometimes eggs. After that, all the shaping and cutting and dyeing is mostly for show. Picking the right pasta shape can help your dish hold the sauce better, and we'll go over that in a second, but those are just suggestions. You are free to mix and match any pasta shape with any sauce or preparation that you want.

I didn't realize this was a big deal to some people until I taught my friend Tracey how to make my favorite tagliatelle with peas and ham (it's phenomenal—don't worry, I'm giving you the recipe at the end of this chapter). She'd never heard of tagliatelle—it's a flat pasta like linguine except it's wider—and was asking me why I had to use that kind of pasta. I told her I didn't, that you could use any pasta you wanted, and she kind of freaked out. "But what does the recipe say?" she wanted to know. "I don't want to make it wrong." There is no wrong way when it comes to picking a pasta shape, I promise. If a recipe gives you a pasta suggestion, it's only a suggestion. Feel free to substitute your favorite noodles, a fun shape you've never tried before, or whatever's on sale that week.

Yes, there are people who think putting a certain sauce on the wrong noodle is like serving a hamburger on a hot dog bun. Get over it! One of the best parts about cooking Italian food is that it's so easy to personalize. I hope that after reading this book you'll be comfortable enough with the ingredients and how to prepare them that you create dozens of your own special recipes! (Although I do want you to name every single one after me or my girls.)

Fresh vs. Dried

Even though they taste almost the same, dried pasta is not just a shriveled version of fresh pasta, like a raisin and a grape. Each type of pasta is made with a different dough and different process. Fresh pasta uses a soft flour and eggs (which give it a little more fat and some cholesterol), and it has to be used immediately or refrigerated. It also costs a little more.

Dried pasta (except for egg noodles, and we do not count egg noodles) is made from a hard durum wheat semolina flour and water. No eggs, no cholesterol. Then it's cut and dried, but it miraculously comes back to soft, doughy life in a pot of hot water. Dried pasta also costs pennies per serving, and it can last years in your pantry.

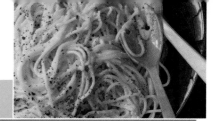

Bronzed Pasta

On some dried pasta packages, especially imported ones, you might see the words *bronze drawn*, or *drawn through a bronze die*. That's a way for companies to tell you they still do things the old-fashioned way.

To make shapes, pasta dough is squeezed through a big press sort of like what you used in grade school to crank out Play-Doh spaghetti. The colored plastic bit that you slid to make different shapes is called a "die," and while it was first made of wood, it's traditionally made of bronze in Italy. Bronze dies give the pasta an almost bumpy edge all around. Many modern companies use plastic dies that make super-smooth pasta.

Either one is fine, but many people prefer the rougher pasta because they say it holds the sauce better and gives your mouth a little more fun because of the texture (ribbed for our pleasure, I guess). In any case, if I can, I usually go for the "party in my mouth" version.

Any pasta that says *rigate* or "ridged" is also telling you it will hold pasta sauce and tickle your tonsils better, but not necessarily because of a bronze die.

It's important to know, though, that dried pasta is not an inferior choice to fresh pasta, like cheese spread you squirt from a can versus fresh cheese. The Italians have been making dried pasta for hundreds of years, and it tastes divine.

Homemade vs. Store-Bought

You know I love to make things from scratch. If I can get my hands into the food, I'm enjoying it before it even hits my mouth. I make my sauces from scratch. Joe makes our sausage from scratch. We even make our own wine. (We don't normally stomp the grapes with our feet and dress like characters from I *Love Lucy*, but this year, me and Jacqueline just had to give it a try. It was too fun.)

Of course, I also know how to make pasta from scratch. Once you know how to do it, you can have fresh pasta ready for cooking in fifteen minutes. But I usually don't, and here's why. The unused pasta doesn't last as long as dried. It creates a whole bunch of extra dishes for me to wash. (And believe me, I've got enough dishes and clothes to wash for the next fifty years. My girls, they gotta change their outfits like three times a day. Drives me crazy!) But the most important reason I don't regularly make my own pasta is because the stuff you can buy in the store is so inexpensive and so good, it's not really worth the extra effort. The difference between homemade sauce and the stuff in a jar? Life-changing! The difference between rolling out your own pasta and the beautiful bags imported from Italy for two dollars? You can't tell.

When I do make my own, though, it's usually for dishes that use big shapes of pasta, like lasagna, manicotti, or ravioli. You roll them out, cut them, and shape them pretty easily. But the small pastas like fusili or farfalle, those I use dried.

Brand Name vs. Generic

In most cases, I choose the products imported from Italy that I know are well made and not full of additives. But for pasta, you can actually go with a local brand, as long as it's a good one.

Mine and Joe's favorite Italian dried pasta brand is De Cecco. It's been made in Abruzzo by the De Cecco family for 120 years. People used to have to dry pasta in the sun until Don Filippo De Cecco invented a drying machine for those rare cloudy days. Their factory was bombed by the Germans in World War Two, but they were able to rebuild because after all the Allied soldiers fell in love with pasta, international demand for their product grew. I also like that they still use a bronze die, and I love their logo: a gorgeous, curvy Abruzzo country girl carrying wheat.

The other dried pasta we usually buy because it tastes fantastic is Via Roma. It sounds all Italian, but it's actually an American brand made by the A&P grocery store. Their packaging is adorable: a black-and-white picture of an elderly couple enjoying a meal. It may be a generic brand, but since A&P gave it a private label and put some thought and skill behind it, it tastes amazing.

I've had friends tell me that the cheapest dried pasta on the shelves doesn't cook up very good. My advice: spend twenty cents more and get a guaranteed winner.

Designer Pasta

Like everything, there are "designer" brands of pasta, called "artisanal pastas," that make smaller batches of better quality and of course charge a bit more for it. But unlike shoes or cars, a box of premium pasta will cost you about seven dollars, rather than two. My favorite is Latini Classica Red Box selection by Carlo and Carla Latini. The Latini family has been farming wheat in Osimo, Italy, since 1888, and they really have perfected it with what they say on their own Web site is "genius and love." They use bronze dies, and their pasta, even in a blind taste test, totally wins, even without any sauce at all. If I'm having fancy visitors I really want to impress, I send Joe down to the Italian market for some Latini. I'm not the only one either, since most of the best Italian restaurants in New York use Latini as well (and you thought they made it all by hand . . . I told you, it's a pain in the ass!).

Specialty Pasta

I said all pasta, fresh or dried, starts out pretty much the same way, as a soft dough. This is true. However, some companies get a little creative and add extra ingredients to their dough. You might see green pasta that has spinach in it. Tricolor pasta. Red pepper or purple beet pasta. In Venice black pasta stained with squid ink is popular!

Colored and flavored pastas are fine, if you like the taste of them; just check the ingredients and make sure the manufacturer didn't add any unwanted extras in there, too. Christmas tree pasta shapes are fun for the holidays, as long as they aren't green only because of an unnatural dye. Look out for added sugar and things like corn syrup, as well.

Whole-Wheat Pasta

The biggest question I get about pasta these days is if I use whole-wheat pasta or not. The answer is: Joe and I tried it, and to be honest, it tasted more like the box it came in than the pasta we were used to.

That was a few years ago, and I hear that the whole-wheat pastas are getting tastier, but I'm still gonna pass on this one. When you make pasta with a whole-wheat flour instead of the hard durum flour, you're changing the consistency the Italians perfected for years and years. I don't need pasta that goes all mushy or won't hold on to the sauce for me.

Pasta is supposed to be an almost silent partner in the dish. It's the vehicle that carries all the rich, fresh ingredients into your mouth. I can't have a pasta with its own strong flavor competing with my perfect toppings.

I did a little research—and by that I mean, I looked at two boxes in the grocery store side-by-side—and I discovered something shocking: all that whole-grain, it's-so-much-healthier-for-you, you've-got-to-switch marketing is complete garbage. Whole-wheat or multigrain or filled-with-wood-chips pasta, whatever you want to call it, has hardly any more fiber

A lot of people want to know if you should use cold water or hot water from the tap to fill your pot for boiling pasta. Either way, it won't affect the pasta. Cold water will take longer to come to a boil, but that's the way we do it.

I don't know if you've ever seen the inside of a used hot-water heater, but I have, and it's not nice in there. Hot water from the faucet doesn't go in my mouth or my family's mouths. Period.

than the regular stuff. Like 2 to 4 grams more. All that fuss and extra expense and dark brown, muddy pasta for 2 extra grams of fiber? No sir! I can make up that extra fiber by eating a quarter cup of raspberries or half an apple. I'll stick to my beloved national dish, thank you very much.

Serving Sizes

One reason Italians can enjoy their pasta every day is because they don't overindulge. America must have the biggest serving spoons in the world, because we just heap mounds of food on our plates.

A good-sized, healthy serving of pasta is one cup of cooked pasta. That's 2 ounces of dried pasta, or 4 ounces when it cooks up. If you want to eat more than that, just plan the rest of your day accordingly. Double up on the spaghetti and cut back on the cheese.

How Fabulous People Cook Pasta

What's the right way to cook pasta? It's a simple question, yet somehow everyone has a different answer. Well, this is my book, and I'm going to give you my answer (which of course is the right one). This is how the most fabulous people in the world do it:

How Fabulous People Cook Pasta!

Step 1 • Use the Right Pot and the Right Amount of Water

For 1 pound of pasta, use a deep, 6- to 8-quart pot. Fill it three quarters full of water. If you use too much water, it will boil over. If you use too little, the pasta won't cook well.

Step 2 • Salt the Water

If you add salt to the water, it won't keep the pasta from sticking, but it will help bring out the flavor of the pasta. (If you're on a salt-sensitive diet, though, for heaven's sake, skip this step!)

However, you have to add the salt at just the right time. If you add it too early, you'll slow down your boil. If you add it too late, the pasta can't absorb it.

As soon as the water has started to boil, add a tablespoon of salt. Let the salt dissolve, and then add the pasta.

Step 3 • Stir the Pot

To keep pasta from sticking together, you want to give it a stir every once in a while. For spaghetti, don't lay it in a clump on one side of the pot. Hold it in the middle of the pot and then open your hand and let it fall to all sides, sort of like an upside-down teepee.

Step 4 • Boil Until Al Dente

Al dente means "to the tooth," and it means the pasta is ready to be drained when it still has a tiny, tiny "bite" to it. Not too firm, but not mushy, either. There is no perfect amount of time because every pasta brand and shape and amount you are cooking will be different. Look at the time recommendations on the box, and start taste-testing from the pot two minutes before you think it's done.

Step 5 • Drain but Do NOT Rinse

As soon as your pasta is finished cooking, drain it in a colander right away. If you leave it in the pot because you're afraid it will get cold, you will have a mushy noodle mess.

Shake the water off the pasta, but don't rinse it at all. I don't know where this rumor started, but if you wash all the starch off it, the sauce won't stick and you'll have a slimy dish.

Step 6 • Don't Use Oil

Italian pasta is perfect on its own. It doesn't need any oil poured over it until you're adding your dressings. If you pour oil over the pasta when it's in the colander, you're basically just pouring money down the sink.

Do You Come Here Often? Famous Pasta Pairings

I know I said you can mix and match whatever pasta with whatever sauce you want. Still true. There are no rules. But for those of you that want to know the most classic pairings, I will help a sister out.

Generally, you put smooth sauces like a marinara on long pasta, and you use shorter shapes with holes and ridges for chunky sauces (so the pasta can cling to the vegetable or meaty bit). Here are some traditional pairings:

- Thick, creamy sauces: usually go on a fettuccine
- Chunky sauces: anything that can hold on to it like cavatappi, orecchiette, or penne
- Seafood sauces: great with linguine
- Really light tomato or oil-based sauce: spaghetti
- Special food you don't want to overwhelm with pasta (like lobster): angel hair is the way to go
- Anything you want your kids to eat: use farfalle
- Great in cold pasta dishes: macaroni, farfalle, rotelle, or rotini
- The best pasta for soups: orzo, ditalini, conchiglie

Pretty Pasta Talk:
No More Bow Ties or Wagon Wheels

Before I leave you with my favorite pasta recipes, I wanted to give you one more little Italian lesson. Pasta shapes are named after things in Italy, so learning the proper name is an easy way to start learning Italian. (And, to be honest, I can't stand in the pasta aisle one more second and hear people mangle the pronunciation!) Here are my favorites. Learn how to say them correctly, and please, please tell all your friends.

CAVATAPPI (CAV-vah-top-pee) • I know there are a million spiral pasta shapes, but *cavatappi* actually means "corkscrew" in Italian. Somehow, there's a way to turn this into a curse word, I just know it . . .

CONCHIGLIE (con-KEEL-yay) • In Italian, this word means "shells," and the pasta is shaped just like shells. This one is a bitch to pronounce, though, if you don't speak Italian, so you're welcome.

DITALINI (dee-tah-LEE-nee) • This adorable pasta means "little thimbles." So yummy in soups!

FARFALLE (far-FALL-lay) • I can kind of see the bow-tie connection (but since when do bow ties have jagged edges?), but *farfalle* means "butterfly" in Italian. Much sweeter, no?

FETTUCCINE (fay-too-CHEE-nay) • In Italian, *fetta* means a "slice" or a "ribbon," so *fettuccine* is "little ribbons."

FUSILLI (foo-ZEE-lee) • *Fusilli* comes from the Italian word for "spindle," which makes sense because these long, spiral noodles used to be formed by hand around knitting needles. My main concern here, though, is that you begin the word with "foo" and not "few."

LINGUINE (lin-GWEEN-ay) • This is a sexy one because *linguetta* means "tongue" in Italian, so you're slurping down "little tongues." (Or maybe they're slurping you . . . ?)

ORECCHIETTE (oh-reck-ee-ET-tay) • I'm going to admit, this pasta shape kind of freaks me out. In Italian, *orecchio* is "ear," so this pasta is really "small ears." And if you look at them, they even have little veins in them and stuff. Kind of creepy. But it does give your mouth a nice massage (and if you can learn to say this one, you'll definitely impress the girls).

RUOTE (roo-OH-tay) and **ROTELLE** (row-TELL-ay) • *Ruote* means "wheels" in Italian, and *rotelle* means "little wheels," so pick one and use it. I never want to hear "wagon wheels" to describe Italian pasta again. (And yes, I know that some pasta companies also use the word *rotelle* on their fat spiral shapes, but I don't care. Just as long as we never use "wagon wheels" again.)

STROZZAPRETTI (stroat-zah-PRAY-tee) • This pasta looks sort of like a small, rolled-up towel, and it's one of my favorites for the name alone. In Italian, it means "priest stranglers." Don't get me wrong; I love priests as much as the next good Italian girl. But according to a legend in Italy, a priest actually suffocated to death while eating this kind of pasta, so they renamed it. I find that kind of hilarious. You'd better have good manners when you eat in Italy, or they might name a pasta after you! (It's worth serving this kind of pasta just to be able to tell the story at the dinner table.)

Perfect Pasta Recipes

All right, Baby Doll, here are my favorite
pasta recipes, from my heart to yours.

TERESA'S FAVORITE TAGLIATELLE

MAKES 6 SERVINGS

This is my absolute favorite pasta dish. If you can't find tagliatelle, you can use linguine. I'll admit it's not necessary to use green pasta since you can't really taste the spinach in it anyway, but I like when it looks all colorful. Feel free to sprinkle a little Parmigiano-Reggiano on top.

**1 pound tagliatelle or linguine pasta,
    preferably 8 ounces each plain and spinach**

3 tablespoons extra virgin olive oil

1 medium onion, chopped

2 garlic cloves, minced

2 tablespoons butter

**5 ounces thick-sliced smoked ham, trimmed of excess fat,
    cut into 1/2-inch cubes**

1 cup cooked fresh or thawed frozen peas

1/4 teaspoon salt

1/8 teaspoon freshly ground black pepper

1. Bring a large pot of lightly salted water to a boil. Add the pasta and cook according to the package directions until al dente. Time the pasta so it is done at about the same time as the sauce.

2. Meanwhile, heat the oil in a medium skillet over medium heat. Add the onion and garlic and cook, stirring occasionally, until the onion is translucent, about 3 minutes. Add the butter and melt. Add the ham and peas and cook, stirring occasionally, until heated through, about 3 minutes more. Reduce the heat to very low to keep warm.

3. Drain the pasta, reserving 1 cup of the pasta cooking water. Return the pasta to the pot. Add the sauce and the salt and pepper. Toss the pasta, adding enough of the pasta water to make a light sauce. Serve hot.

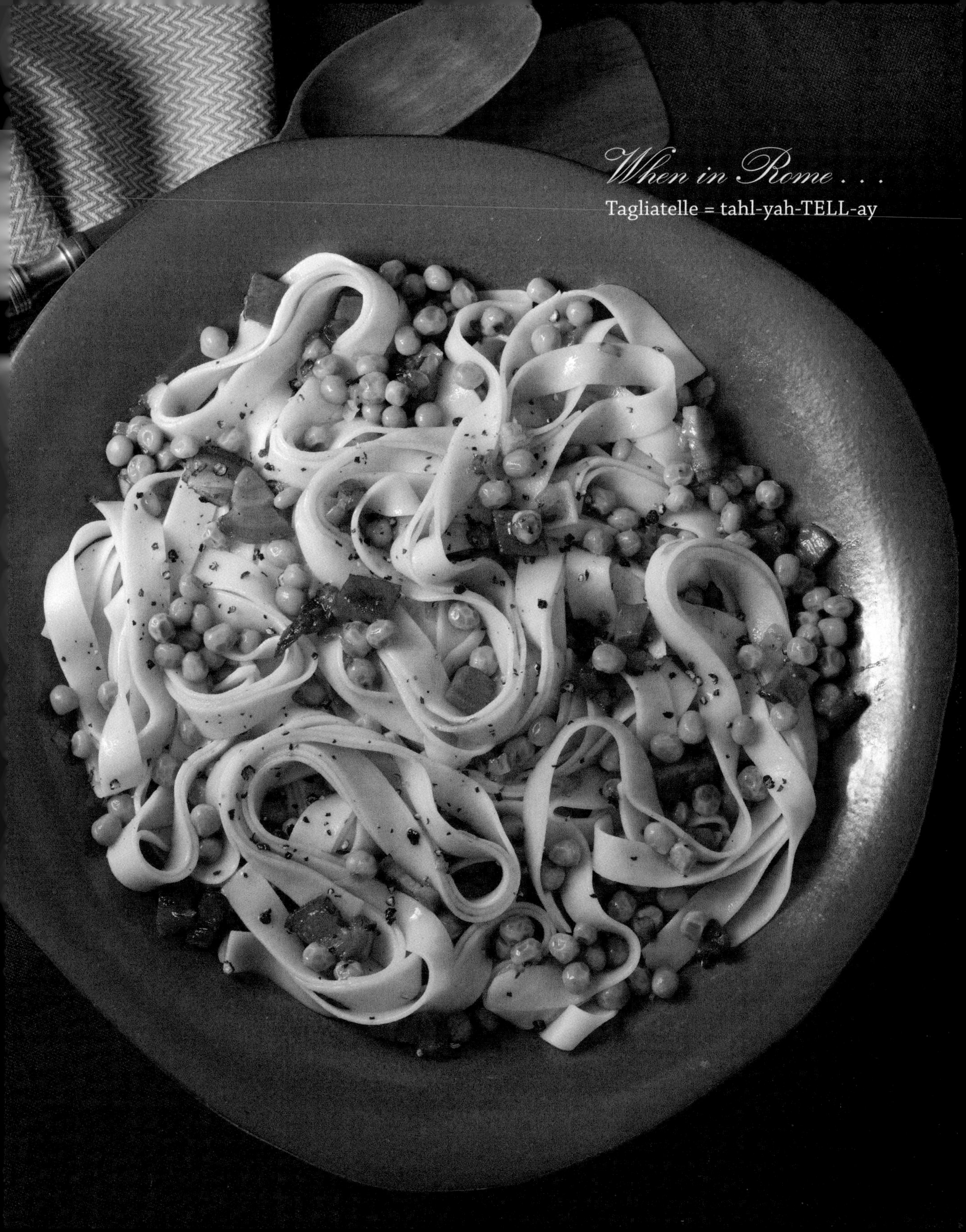

When in Rome . . .

Tagliatelle = tahl-yah-TELL-ay

Italian Bacon ❦

Just as Americans think everything tastes better with bacon, Italians love their pork products: specifically *prosciutto*, *pancetta*, and *guanciale*. Prosciutto (pro-SHOO-toe), the most common in America, is really just a dry-cured ham, sliced really thin and served uncooked, usually as an appetizer. Pancetta (pan-CHET-tuh) is the closest to bacon (it's from the same cut), but it's not smoked like bacon. Guanciale (gwan-CHA-lay) is very similar to pancetta, although it has more collagen that melts into sauces and makes them very silky. Guanciale is harder to find in regular supermarkets, but you can find it in Italian delis or even online. Unless you grew up in Umbria or Lazio, though, you probably won't be able to taste the difference between pancetta and guanciale, so feel free to use whichever you can find. But don't substitute bacon! Its smoky flavor will overpower and change your beautiful Italian dish.

BUCATINI ALL'AMATRICIANA

This pasta is one of the most popular dishes in Italy, especially in Rome, although it comes from the town of Amatrice in central Italy. It's a variation of an old shepherds' dish, and like most of the food that was originally eaten by working people on the go, it's simple, filling, and sooo delicious!

If you can't find bucatini, you can use perciatelli or a really thick spaghetti instead.

1 pound bucatini or perciatelli pasta

2 tablespoons extra virgin olive oil

4 ounces thick-sliced guanciale or pancetta, cut into 1/2-inch pieces

1 medium onion, finely chopped

4 ripe plum tomatoes, seeded and cut into 1/2-inch dice

1/2 teaspoon salt

1/8 teaspoon crushed hot red pepper

1/2 cup freshly grated Pecorino Romano

1. Bring a large pot of lightly salted water to a boil over high heat. Add the bucatini and cook according to the package directions until almost al dente, but slightly undercooked. Time the pasta so it is done at about the same time as the sauce.

2. Meanwhile, heat the oil in a large skillet over medium heat. Add the guanciale and cook, stirring occasionally, until browned, about 5 minutes. Using a slotted spoon, transfer the meat to paper towels to drain, leaving the fat in the skillet.

3. Add the onion to the skillet and cook, stirring occasionally, until translucent, about 3 minutes. Add the tomatoes, salt, and hot pepper and cook, stirring occasionally, until the tomatoes have given off their juices, about

5 minutes. Return the guanciale to the skillet, remove from the heat, and cover to keep warm.

4. Drain the pasta. Return the pasta to the pot and add the sauce. Cook over low heat, stirring often, until the pasta is coated with sauce and just al dente, about 1 minute. Remove from the heat, add the cheese, and toss. Serve hot.

• • •

FARFALLE CON PISELLI

MAKES 6 SERVINGS

My kids love this dish because it's so pretty: butterflies (farfalle) and peas (piselli) in a creamy sauce. Yes, we are using cream here, but it's less than one tablespoon per serving, so you get a lot of flavor for a minimal amount of fat and calories.

1 pound farfalle pasta

1 tablespoon extra virgin olive oil

1 medium onion, chopped

1 garlic clove, finely chopped

1 cup cooked fresh or thawed frozen peas

1/3 cup light cream

1/4 teaspoon salt

1/8 teaspoon freshly ground black pepper

1 tablespoon chopped fresh parsley

1. Bring a large pot of lightly salted water to a boil over high heat. Add the farfalle and cook according to the package directions until just tender. Time the pasta so it is done at about the same time as the sauce.

2. Meanwhile, heat the oil in a medium skillet over medium heat. Add

the onion and garlic and cook, stirring occasionally, until tender but not browned, about 5 minutes. Add the peas, cream, salt, and pepper and bring to a boil. Remove from the heat and cover to keep warm.

3. Drain the pasta well. Return the pasta to the pot. Add the sauce and toss well. Sprinkle with the parsley and serve hot.

PASTA CACIO E PEPE

MAKES 6 SERVINGS

I love this recipe because it's classically Italian: simple, just a few ingredients, the pasta isn't drowning in a sauce, and it's so filling. Cacio is cheese (and this recipe is only made with Pecorino Romano) and pepe is black pepper. My dad is allergic to black pepper, so when he's over, we substitute hot pepper flakes. Just as good, but a little spicier!

1 pound spaghetti

2 cups (8 ounces) freshly grated Pecorino Romano

¼ teaspoon salt

½ teaspoon freshly ground black pepper

When in Rome . . .

Cacio = CACH-oh

1. Bring a large pot of lightly salted water to a boil over high heat. Add the spaghetti and cook according to the package directions until al dente. Drain well, reserving 1 cup of the pasta water.

2. Return the pasta to the pot. Add the cheese, salt, and pepper. Toss the pasta, gradually adding enough of the pasta water to make a smooth sauce. Serve hot.

PENNE WITH
PORTOBELLO MUSHROOM SAUCE

MAKES 6 SERVINGS

I love portobello mushrooms, and this dish is great on cold nights; even its earthy brown color just makes you feel all warm inside. The longer you cook the mushrooms, the more taste you will get out of them.

3 large portobello mushrooms

2 tablespoons extra virgin olive oil

2 garlic cloves, minced

1 small red bell pepper, cored, seeded, and cut into $1/2$-inch dice

$1/4$ teaspoon salt

$1/8$ teaspoon freshly ground black pepper

$1/4$ cup red wine vinegar

1 pound penne

$1/2$ cup freshly grated Parmigiano-Reggiano

1. Rinse the mushrooms well. Trim off any hard parts. Cut off the stems and cut them into $1/2$-inch dice. Slice the caps in half crosswise, then into $1/4$-inch-thick strips.

2. Heat the oil in a large skillet over medium heat. Add the mushrooms and half of the minced garlic. Cover and cook, stirring occasionally, until the mushrooms are tender, about 20 minutes. Stir in the bell pepper, remaining garlic, salt, and black pepper. Cook, uncovered, stirring occasionally, until the bell pepper is tender, about 8 minutes more. Stir in the vinegar and cook for 1 minute. Remove from the heat and cover to keep warm.

3. Meanwhile, bring a large pot of lightly salted water to a boil over high heat. Add the spaghetti and cook according to the package directions until al dente. Drain well, reserving $1/2$ cup of the pasta water.

4. Return the pasta to the pot. Add the mushroom mixture and toss, adding enough of the pasta water to make a slightly moist sauce. Sprinkle with the cheese, toss again, and serve hot.

7 ✖ The Secret's in the Sauce

If there's one thing I love, it's the *top*: over-the-top, top-shelf, top-rated, top-selling . . . everything is yummiest when it's on the top. (And I know you know what I mean.)

It's the dressing that makes salad come alive. Strawberries turn magical when covered with Sambuca. And a cappuccino without the foam is just a plain old cup of coffee.

The same is true of Italian sauces. A good sauce would make a leather shoe taste delicious. Every Italian cook worth her salt needs to have at the very least one homemade sauce in her repertoire. And since tomatoes are a nutritious "superfood," good for your heart, skin, and mind, let's start with a tomato sauce.

The Chef Boyardee Problem

Too many Americans think "tomato sauce" is the finished product you throw over spaghetti. *Uffa!* Tomato sauce is the base you need to prepare dozens of other tomato-based Italian sauces (also commonly called "red sauces").

Using pasta from a box instead of making it from scratch is perfectly fine, but there is no excuse for using tomato sauce from the store. If you use a store-bought sauce, you're not only robbing yourself of most of the natural antioxidants (and adding unnecessary chemicals into your body), but you are ruining your taste buds (and, quite possibly, your reputation).

And do I even have to say it? *Pasta* doesn't come in a can. Never, ever, ever.

Italian red sauces have two or three parts: the *soffrito* (or the light frying of vegetables in olive oil), the tomato sauce, and the (optional) meat.

Homemade Tomato Sauce Recipe

Once a year, I make jars and jars of homemade tomato sauce so I always have some sitting around, ready to be used in an exquisite red sauce, at a moment's notice. Canning ahead of time isn't that hard (I'll teach you how in Chapter 9), but it's also not a requirement to serve a quick, delicious dinner. You can easily whip up a homemade tomato sauce in a matter of minutes. In fact, the recipe is so simple, I call it "The Quickie." You'll make this first, then set it aside, and add it to the other recipes whenever they need a Quickie.

Breaking Tomatoes

For any red sauce, you have to first break up the tomatoes into pieces or they won't melt into a sauce. What size pieces? About the size of a big stuffed olive. And I always include the juices in the can because they add flavor and moisture to any dish.

There are a few ways to break your tomatoes. (One way not to do it is to chop the tomatoes on your chopping board—what a freakin' mess!) You could pulse the contents of the can in a food processor until the tomatoes are coarsely chopped. Or, you can insert clean kitchen scissors into the can and snip the tomatoes into chunks.

But the easiest way is the time-honored, hands-on method. With one hand, hold the can right over the saucepan, so when the juices squirt, they hit the sides of the pan and not you. Reach your other (clean) hand right into the can (make sure there aren't any sharp edges from removing the lid), and as you pour the tomatoes and the juices into the saucepan, squish and squeeze the chunks as they slide out.

Basic Tomato Sauce, aka "The Quickie"

1 tablespoon extra virgin olive oil

One 28-ounce can imported Italian plum tomatoes,
 broken up, with their juices

1/4 cup tomato paste

2 tablespoons chopped fresh basil or 2 teaspoons dried basil

MAKES ABOUT
3 1/2 CUPS, ENOUGH FOR
1 POUND OF PASTA

1. Heat the oil in a large saucepan over medium heat. Add the tomatoes and their juices and the tomato paste. Bring just to a boil.

2. Reduce the heat to medium-low and add the basil. Simmer to blend the flavors, about 10 minutes. The end.

When in Rome . . .
Marinara = mar-ree-NAR-ra

Sauces to Cry For

Now that you have a true tomato sauce, you are ready to make dozens of delicious sauces. I'm going to give you my family recipes for five tomato sauce–based classics—Marinara, Bolognese, Puttanesca, Napoletano, and Arrabbiata—but you'll soon discover you can create your own signature sauce with a good tomato sauce and your favorite seasonings. I'm naming the sauces after my kids, because my kids are gorgeous and delicious, and I could just eat them up.

MILANIA'S MARINARA SAUCE

Marinara sauce is what most people think of as the classic Italian red spaghetti sauce. And it is great over spaghetti, but you can use it over any pasta. It's nice and light, and super healthy, so enjoy your spaghetti guilt-free!

MAKES ABOUT
3 ½ CUPS, ENOUGH FOR
1 POUND OF PASTA

1 tablespoon extra virgin olive oil

12 cremini mushrooms, sliced

1 medium onion, finely chopped

2 garlic cloves, minced

3 ½ cups "The Quickie" Tomato Sauce (see page 117)

½ cup hearty red wine

1 ½ teaspoons dried oregano

¼ teaspoon salt

¼ teaspoon freshly ground black pepper or crushed hot red pepper

1. Heat the oil in a large saucepan over medium-high heat. Add the mushrooms and cook, stirring often, until they are beginning to brown, about 5 minutes. Move the mushrooms to one side of the saucepan. Add the onion to the empty side of the saucepan and cook, stirring the onion occasionally,

continues on page 120

Sauce of the Sailors

"Marinara": it sounds so good, I almost wish it were a girl's name because I'd use it! But it's not. "Marinara" is from the Italian word *marinaro*, which means "of the sea."

Marinara sauce was first favored by the sailors in Naples in the sixteenth century and so it was named "the sauce of the sailors."

The ships' cooks loved it because as a tomato-based sauce without any meat or seafood in it, it could last for long voyages without needing refrigeration (which, of course, they didn't have on boats back then).

until it softens, about 2 minutes. Add the garlic, stir everything together, and cook until the onion is tender, about 2 minutes more.

2. Stir in the tomato sauce, wine, oregano, salt, and pepper and bring to a simmer. Reduce the heat to medium-low. Simmer, uncovered, stirring occasionally, until the sauce is thickened and well flavored, at least 30 minutes and up to 4 hours, but the longer the better! If the sauce gets too thick, add a little water. Serve hot, as a pasta sauce.

• • •

GABRIELLA'S BOLOGNESE SAUCE

MAKES ABOUT 6 CUPS, ENOUGH FOR 2 POUNDS OF PASTA

Teresa's
T·I·P

To save time, use a food processor to chop, dice, and mince your vegetables and meats.

Bolognese sauce is a meat-based sauce originally from Bologna, Italy. It traditionally uses less tomato sauce than other recipes (especially a marinara), and at least two different kinds of ground meat ("minced meat" to the rest of the world). I like it best over cavatelli pasta (the pasta that looks like little hot dog buns), but any pasta that can grab onto the sauce is good.

I make this sauce for Dina Manzo all the time. She's like one of those carnivores who has to have meat at every meal. I love meat, but no one loves meat like Dina. (She's going to kill me for saying that because it sounds all sexy and stuff, but it's the truth. And she is all sexy and stuff.)

1 tablespoon extra virgin olive oil

1 medium onion, chopped

1/2 carrot, cut into 1/2-inch dice

1/2 celery rib, cut into 1/2-inch dice

1 garlic clove, minced

8 ounces ground pork

8 ounces ground veal

3 ¹/₂ cups "The Quickie" Tomato Sauce (see page 117)

1 cup dry white wine

3 tablespoons chopped fresh parsley

¹/₂ teaspoon salt

¹/₄ teaspoon freshly ground black pepper

When in Rome . . .
Bolognese = bow-lone-YAY-say
Napoletano = nah-pole-lay-TAWN-oh

1. Heat the oil in a large saucepan over medium heat. Add the onion, carrot, celery, and garlic. Cook, stirring occasionally, until the onion is translucent, about 5 minutes.

2. Add the pork and veal and cook, breaking up the meat with the side of a spoon, until the meat loses its raw look, about 5 minutes.

3. Stir in the tomato sauce, wine, parsley, salt, and pepper and bring to a simmer. Reduce the heat to medium-low. Simmer, uncovered, stirring occasionally, until the sauce is thickened and well flavored, at least 30 minutes and up to 2 hours, the longer the better! Serve hot, as a pasta sauce.

GIA'S NAPOLETANO SAUCE

MAKES ABOUT 5 CUPS, ENOUGH FOR 1 ¹/₂ POUNDS OF PASTA

Like Bolognese, Napoletano is named for the city it comes from: Naples. (You might see it as Neapolitan Sauce in America.) The biggest difference between the two sauces is that Bolognese uses ground meat and less onion and tomato sauce, while Napoletano uses whole meat or meatballs. Napoletano sauce is typically what Italians serve at their weekend family dinners, and it's also called "Sunday gravy." It would sit on the back of the stove simmering for hours while everyone went to Mass. When you got home, the smell . . . unbelievable!

You can make this with different meats—Italian sausage and pork shoulder is really popular—but I try to pick healthier meats (and save the sausage for dishes where it's the star!). Some cooks even use chicken.

continues on page 122

Napoletano is a
great sauce to make
ahead of time. And
it freezes well, too.
Make more than
you need, and
freeze leftover sauce
(meat and all) for
future lasagnas,
eggplant dishes,
even to spread
over pizza!

There are hundreds of variations on this recipe, but this one came over from Italy with my mamma, and it's the best.

**1 ½ pounds beef top round steak (about ⅛ inch thick),
   cut into 4 equal pieces**

4 pork spareribs, preferably in one piece, but individual ribs are OK

1 ½ teaspoons salt

¾ teaspoon freshly ground black pepper

⅓ cup finely chopped fresh parsley

¼ cup freshly grated Pecorino Romano

2 tablespoons extra virgin olive oil

1 medium onion, chopped

½ cup hearty red wine

3 ½ cups "The Quickie" Tomato Sauce (see page 117)

1. Pat the round steak and spareribs dry with paper towels. Season with 1 teaspoon salt and ½ teaspoon pepper. Mix the parsley and Pecorino Romano cheese together in a shallow dish. Pat and rub the cheese mixture into the meats.

2. Heat 1 tablespoon of the oil in a large saucepan over medium heat. In batches without crowding, add the meat and cook, turning occasionally, until browned, about 5 minutes. Adjust the heat so the meat browns nicely without burning. You want little chunks stuck to the bottom of the pan, as these will help flavor the sauce. Transfer the meat to a plate.

3. Heat the remaining oil in the saucepan. Add the onion and cook, stirring occasionally, until translucent, about 5 minutes. Increase the heat to high and add the wine. Cook, stirring up the browned chunks in the bottom of the saucepan (the fancy word for this is *deglazing*; yeah, I didn't know that either). Bring to a boil.

4. Stir in the tomato sauce, 1 cup water, and the remaining ½ teaspoon salt and ¼ teaspoon pepper. Return the beef and pork to the saucepan and bring to a simmer. Reduce the heat to medium-low. Partially cover the

saucepan. Simmer, stirring occasionally, until the meat is very tender, about 1 3/4 hours.

5. Remove the meats from the sauce and transfer to a cutting board. Cut the beef into 1/2-inch pieces. Cut the meat from the spareribs, discard the bones, and coarsely chop the pork. Return the meats to the sauce. Serve hot, as a pasta sauce.

• • •

DANIELLE'S PUTTANESCA SAUCE

OK, I don't have a daughter named Danielle, but I couldn't name this dish after any one of my darling girls. It's delicious, and very popular in our house, but the name . . . the name . . . First let's cook it, and then I'll tell you why I could only name it for a grown woman.

This sauce is usually poured over spaghetti, but you can use any noodle you want.

MAKES ABOUT 3 3/4 CUPS, ENOUGH FOR 1 POUND OF PASTA

> 2 tablespoons extra virgin olive oil
>
> 3 garlic cloves, minced
>
> 2 teaspoons anchovy paste
>
> 1/2 teaspoon crushed hot red pepper
>
> 3 1/2 cups "The Quickie" Tomato Sauce (see page 117)
>
> 1/2 cup pitted and coarsely chopped kalamata olives
>
> 2 tablespoons drained capers

1. Pour the oil into a large saucepan. Add the garlic, anchovy paste, and hot pepper and cook over medium heat, stirring often, until the garlic is very fragrant and beginning to turn golden brown, about 2 minutes.

2. Stir in the tomato sauce, olives, and capers and bring to a simmer. Reduce the heat to medium-low. Simmer, uncovered, stirring occasionally, until lightly thickened, about 15 minutes. Serve hot, as a pasta sauce.

When in Rome . . .
Puttanesca = pooh-tah-NES-kah

Pasta Puttanesca is a common dish in Italy, where it enjoys an uncommon name: "whore's spaghetti." It was supposedly invented in the 1950s when brothels were owned and run by the Italian government (a way to keep them under control, I guess). The brothels were required to have their shutters closed at all times to shield the good Italian women on the street from having to look at the *puttanas*, or prostitutes. The "ladies of the evening" were only allowed out for a short amount of time to shop in the local markets, so they had to quickly grab whatever they could. Pasta Puttanesca was their meal of choice because it was cheap and could be made in a jiffy, between customers.

An Italian restaurant owner in the 1950s also claims to have invented the dish for his hungry friends late one night, saying he named it after *puttanata*, the Italian word for "garbage." In either case, the name fits.

ARRABBIATA, THE ANGRY SAUCE

I'm a pretty laid-back person, but certain things piss me off. Pathological puttanas, *for one. So now seems like the perfect time to introduce Arrabbiata, the spiciest of Italian sauces.*

Now, I like it hot, but if you want to tone it down, only use ¹/2 teaspoon of the red pepper flakes. I like it best over penne, but some people use linguine or spaghetti.

MAKES ABOUT
3 ³/4 CUPS, ENOUGH FOR
1 POUND OF PASTA

1 tablespoon extra virgin olive oil

¹/2 medium onion, chopped

4 garlic cloves, finely chopped

1 teaspoon crushed hot red pepper

3 ¹/2 cups "The Quickie" Tomato Sauce (see page 117)

1 tablespoon fresh lemon juice

¹/2 teaspoon freshly ground black pepper

2 tablespoons chopped fresh parsley

1. Heat the oil in a large saucepan over medium heat. Add the onion and garlic and cook, stirring occasionally, until the onion is translucent, about 5 minutes. Stir in the hot pepper.

2. Stir in the tomato sauce, lemon juice, and pepper. Bring to a simmer. Reduce the heat to medium-low. Simmer, uncovered, stirring occasionally, until lightly thickened, at least 15 and up to 40 minutes. The longer it simmers, the hotter the sauce. If the sauce gets too thick, stir in a little water. Just before serving, stir in the parsley. Serve hot, as a pasta sauce.

When in Rome . . .
Arrabbiata = ah-rah-BYAH-tah

Arrabbiata is the Italian word for "angry." What's the tie-in with pasta sauce? Maybe your mouth gets mad that the sauce is so hot (well, not my mouth, but maybe your mouth . . .).

Now, this is the first, last, and only time I want to hear anything about *The Sopranos*, but if any of you remember, Tony gave one of his bodyguards, Perry Annunziata, the nickname "Penne Arrabbiata" because the guy had such a hot temper. So now you're in on the joke. (It was in Season Six if you want to watch it. Good episode.)

Have I been called "Joe Arrabbiata" before? Sure. You could easily add "Arrabbiata" to the name of just about every Italian I know—Teresa and all her friends included!

Slow-Cooker Sauce Shortcuts

Since most Italian sauces only taste better the longer they simmer, ideally, you should have a saucepan sitting on the back burner pretty much all day long. But for those of us with small children (or a fear of burning down the house), leaving a large, uncovered pot of hot sauce around isn't so practical.

I'm not a big slow-cooker person; I usually only use my Crock-Pot to keep sauces hot when I'm having a party. But they come in super handy when you want to keep a sauce a'simmering.

Just prepare any recipe like you normally would, in a saucepan, until it comes to the simmering stage. Then pour (or ladle, if you tend to be a sloppy pourer like me and don't want a hot mess) the sauce into your slow cooker. Set it, forget it, and you'll have an even better sauce (tucked safely away in the corner of the counter) with half the worry.

Who Is This "Alfredo" and
What Has He Done to My Sauce?

Now that we've covered my favorite red sauces, I want to give you the recipes for the best other colored sauces: white and green.

When I ask you to picture a classic Italian "white" sauce, I bet you immediately think of the sauce served on fettuccine Alfredo in restaurants across the country. Creamy and white, right? More like gluey, gooey, and a heart attack on a plate! Gagging . . .

Prepare yourself: there is no such thing as Alfredo sauce in Italy. Alfredo is a big, fat, American lie. A lie you're best to forget you ever knew, as there is nothing remotely redeeming about it. It drowns the pasta. It makes your stomach feel like it's filled with cement. I know I'm being harsh on the sauce, and maybe you've enjoyed it before, but stop. Now. It's not Italian, and it's *so* not healthy. You might as well eat a stick of butter coated in lard, deep-fried in funnel-cake batter . . . with a cigarette.

The true "white" sauce in Italy is known as *pasta bianco* ("pasta in white") in the southern regions, and *pasta al burro* ("pasta with butter") in the north. Traditionally, before the tomato was introduced to Italy, cheese was the normal topping of pasta dishes, followed by oils and herbs. Butter was also used, although nowhere near as much as people put in their American dishes. An Italian white sauce has nothing in it but cheese, butter, and maybe a little pepper or parsley. Light and delicious.

In 1914, a restaurant owner in Rome, Alfredo di Lelio, supposedly created his own version of the traditional *pasta al burro* by tripling the amount of butter used. His wife was pregnant at the time and couldn't keep food down (I never had that problem, but I have lots of friends who, no matter how sick they were when they were pregnant, could still manage to eat butter). The extra butter did the trick, his wife started eating again, and Alfredo added his *al burro* sauce to his menu. Thirteen years later, in 1927, silent film stars Mary Pickford and Douglas Fairbanks ate at the Roman restaurant while on their honeymoon, and they fell in love with the white sauce. The resulting media frenzy (kind of like when Brad Pitt and Angelina Jolie are photographed at the McDonald's drive-through) traveled to America, where everyone tried to copy "Alfredo's" sauce. Not able to re-create the creamy butter found in Italy, or find the exact kind of cheese, American cooks added cream, extra butter, and even egg yolks to the sauce, and kindly named the sloppy mess after poor Alfredo. (Don't feel sorry for him, though. He went on to own a bunch of restaurants, even one at Disney World.)

I'm going to teach you how to make the delicious *pasta al burro*, because you just can't eat another serving of the bastardized version. According to their own nutritional guide, a serving of fettuccine Alfredo at the Olive Garden has 1,220 calories and 75 grams of fat (47 grams of the evilest of all, saturated fat!). Traditional *pasta al burro* has almost one third of the calories and half the fat content (plus it tastes way better). I'm going to go one better, and give you my own special skinny version.

SKINNY PASTA AL BURRO

MAKES 6 SERVINGS

The deliciousness of this dish is directly related to the quality of the ingredients you use. Don't think regular Parmesan cheese will cut it. You have to get the best Parmigiano-Reggiano cheese you can find (aged twenty-four months is perfection). You can also use other pastas besides fettuccine. My kids love this with penne (much more fork friendly!).

> 3 tablespoons extra virgin olive oil
>
> 2 tablespoons unsalted butter, at room temperature
>
> 1 pound fettuccine, preferably fresh
>
> ¼ teaspoon salt
>
> ¼ teaspoon freshly ground black pepper
>
> Large pinch of minced fresh parsley
>
> ½ cup (2 ounces) freshly grated Parmigiano-Reggiano

continues on page 130

1. Bring a large pot of lightly salted water to a boil over high heat.

2. Meanwhile, heat the oil and butter together in a large saucepan over medium heat until the butter is melted. Remove from the heat.

3. Add the fettuccine to the water and cook according to the package instructions until al dente. Fresh pasta cooks really quickly, so don't overcook it. Drain, reserving about ¼ cup of the pasta cooking water.

4. Transfer the fettuccine to the saucepan with the butter mixture. Add the salt, pepper, and parsley. Return the saucepan to low heat. Toss, adding enough of the pasta water to make a glossy sauce that isn't watery or gluey. Remove from the heat, sprinkle with the cheese, and serve immediately.

● ● ●

It's Easy Being Green

The last great sauce you need in your recipe box is pesto. The tasty green sauce was invented in the Liguria region of Italy (if you think of Italy as a boot, Liguria is the top front, where you would put your hands to slip it on your foot; basically the northwest coastline).

Ligurians have been making pesto since Roman times, although it only became popular in the United States in the 1980s. The creamy basil and garlic sauce is a big part of the Ligurians' healthy diet. (Ligurians live longer than almost anyone else on the planet, beaten only by the Japanese and the Icelanders. With all due respect, I'd much rather eat bread and pesto my whole life than cold fish!)

Pesto comes from *pestare*, the Italian word for "pound" or "bruise." That's because, traditionally, pesto is made with a mortar and pestle (the heavy little bowl and the fun, *National Geographic*–like stick with a rounded end). Even though you can make pesto in a food processor, the flavors are best if you hand-crush them because you want the basil leaves bruised and juiced, not pureed.

I named this last sauce after my newest baby: Audriana. She's gorgeous, of course, and not the least bit green, but I did feel a little bruised after she came out, so there you go.

AUDRIANA'S PESTO

There are dozens of variations, and you can play around and add your own choice of herbs, nuts, or cheeses. Here's my favorite pesto recipe, fresh from the Italian Riviera.

MAKES 1 CUP, ENOUGH FOR 2 POUNDS OF PASTA

$1/3$ cup pine nuts

$1 1/2$ cups packed fresh basil leaves, well rinsed and dried in a salad spinner

3 garlic cloves, crushed under a knife and peeled

$2/3$ cup extra virgin olive oil

$1/2$ cup freshly grated Parmigiano-Reggiano

$1/4$ teaspoon salt

$1/8$ teaspoon freshly ground black pepper

1. Heat a small skillet over medium heat. Add the pine nuts and cook, stirring often, until lightly toasted, 2 to 3 minutes. Transfer to a plate and cool completely.

2. To make the pesto by hand, crush a handful of the basil leaves in a large mortar (at least 2-cup capacity), pushing down with the pestle and moving your wrist in a circular movement to squeeze and crush, but not pound, the leaves. Keep adding basil leaves until they have all been crushed. Add the garlic and crush it into the mixture. Gradually work in about half of the oil. Now add the pine nuts, and crush them in. Finally, work in the cheese, then the remaining oil. Season with the salt and pepper.

3. To make the pesto in a food processor, fit the processor with the metal chopping blade. With the machine running, drop the garlic through the feed tube to mince the garlic. Add the pine nuts and pulse until finely chopped. Add the basil and pulse until finely chopped. Add the cheese and pulse to combine. With the machine running, gradually pour in the oil. Season with the salt and pepper. *continues on page 133*

4. Transfer the pesto to a small covered container. Pour a small amount of oil over the surface of the pesto to seal it. Cover and refrigerate for up to 1 month. Stir well before using.

Note: To use the pesto as a sauce for pasta, boil 1 pound of pasta (linguine or spaghetti are nice) according to the package directions until al dente. Drain, reserving ½ cup of the pasta cooking liquid. Return the pasta to the pot. Add ½ cup pesto and toss, adding enough of the pasta liquid to loosen the pesto and coat the pasta. Season again with salt and pepper and serve hot.

Teresa's
T·I·P

To save time later, make two batches of pesto at once, and freeze half of it. Pour the pesto into an ice-cube tray, and once the cubes are frozen, pop them out into little zippered freezer bags. That way, they are easier to store, and you always have pesto ready to go. (Especially great when you want to pop some pesto in a great soup!)

Sauce vs. Gravy

It's a hot debate in the Italian-American community as to whether you call stuff we put over pasta "sauce" or "gravy." There's even a group on Facebook with eight thousand members called "Real Italians call it gravy, not sauce."

As you know, I'm a real Italian, and I can settle this once and for all. Real Italians don't call it either one. The Italians use either the word *sugo* or *salsa*. Somewhere during the trip across the Atlantic to our wonderful American melting pot, the words got translated into "sauce" in some households, and "gravy" in others. There's really no difference between the two words. We're all referring to the same thing. It's just a matter of personal preference what you were raised calling it.

Still, I'm always asked which word we say in the Giudice house: sauce or gravy. People especially wanna know since most Italians in New Jersey call it "gravy." Well, in case you couldn't tell from the eighty-five times I used the word in this chapter, we call it "sauce" in my house.

You say tomato. I say tomato. It's all the best topping in the world!

8 Pizza! Pizza!

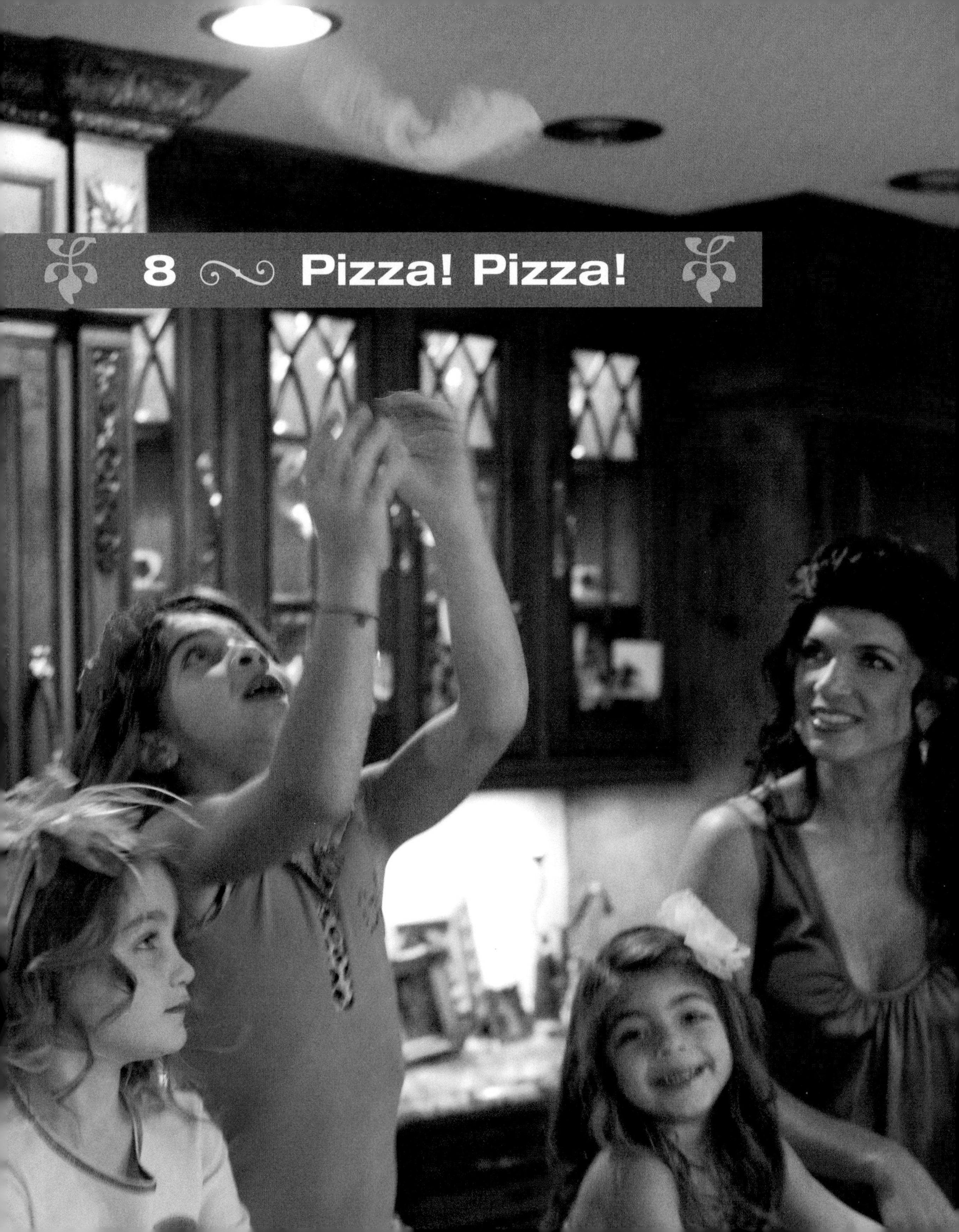

Pizza is one of the most loved foods on the planet because it can include all the food groups (and then some!); it fills you up; you can personalize it with what you like (or pick off what you don't); it's good hot or cold, fresh or leftover; it's easy and cheap to make; and it's very transportable. Almost every country in the world has its own version of pizza, even Pakistan. In Japan, they eat eel pizza. They put sweet potatoes on it in Korea. Coconut goes on pies in Costa Rica. And in Australia, I'm not even kidding, they eat their pizza with kangaroo and crocodile on top.

But no one does it like the original creators: the Italians. If you've ever been to Italy, to Naples specifically, and had true, authentic Italian pizza, you know what I'm talking about. If you've never been, Italian pizza is beyond the best; it's like nothing you've ever tasted. It melts in your mouth; it's light and crispy, yet still doughy and chewy. It's mind-blowing. The good news is my parents brought a lot of their pizza secrets back from Salerno, and we're going to teach you how to make the best Italian pizza this side of the Atlantic.

Beware the Mascot with a Fat Ass

Before we begin, a quick word on what pizza is, or, more importantly, what it isn't. True Italian pizza is a thin, rustic flatbread with fresh toppings on it, very little cheese, and rarely fatty meats. The American version is a little dif-

ferent: it's an orgy of processed cheese, artery-clogging grease, and more bread than you should eat in a month. Yes, it might taste good, but it's not good for you. Even the mascots of American pizza companies are little fat guys. I'm pretty sure I don't want to eat something that advertises right on their neon sign that I'm going to get a fat ass from it. Let me teach you how to make something just as delicious that won't actually take years off your life.

A Brief History of Pie

The first thing you must know is pizza was invented in Italy. I don't want to hear any of that garbage about its being invented in China or Greece. Every civilization since Moses has had a flat bread. It's a pretty simple thing to invent, and very good for an age without refrigerators but with plenty of fire. People used to bake dough on hot rocks. Soldiers in ancient Rome cooked flat bread on their shields in the sun. Greeks had the pita. And they did have this green-onion pancake thing in China. But Marco Polo didn't take it back to Italy with him. Italians already had their own flat breads, and, like everywhere else in the world, were covering them with local ingredients.

The modern pizza as we know it (not the American version, but the Italian version) was first created in Naples, as a food peddled to poor people in the streets. Antica Pizzeria Port'Alba in Naples began making pizzas for the street vendors in the early 1700s and finally opened their own restaurant in 1830, the world's first pizzeria. (It's still open, serving pizza today. If you can get there, it is definitely worth it! *Madonna mia*, is it good!)

Even though we call this first modern pizza a Neapolitan pizza, in Naples, they only consider two kinds of pizza to be true Neapolitan: Marinara and Margherita. There's even an association with specific rules about how to make it if you want to call it a Neapolitan pizza: the dough has to be kneaded by hand, no machines or even rolling pins can be used; it has to be baked in a domed, wood-burning oven at a scorching 905°F for no more than ninety seconds; and the pizza can't be larger than 13.7 inches in diameter, or thicker than 3 millimeters at the center. Thankfully, I'm not that picky. Let me show you how my parents, Antonia and Giacinto Gorda, made it in the Old World (and how they still make it my kitchen today).

Four Steps to Great Homemade Pizza

Just like a good red sauce, you've got to know how to make your own pizza from scratch. This might look like a lot of information, but that's only because I want to give you every single tip for preparing it the first time. Once you've done it, you'll be able to whip up a pie in your kitchen, no problem!

Step 1 • Preheating the Pizza Stone

At least thirty minutes before you're ready to bake your pizza, place a pizza stone on the lowest rack of your oven, and heat the oven to 475°F. (If you don't have a pizza stone, you can cook the pizza on the back of a baking pan, but you don't need to preheat the pan. Only the stone needs to get good and hot.) You can leave the pizza stone in the oven, even if you aren't baking pizza. Just be careful not to spill on the stone, as once it gets dirty, it can smoke and smell up the kitchen. It's a good idea to place the baking dish on a baking sheet to catch any drips.

I've been in construction and working with stone from Italy for some years now. And a pizza stone is literally just that: a stone. So, do you need one? It depends. All pizza used to be cooked on stone, so if you're looking for a really good Italian pie with a nice crisp crust, then the pizza stone's the way to go. The stone works because you get it hot in the oven before you put the pizza on it, and the stone has little holes in it, so it can suck out the moisture of the dough and give the crust a nice, crispy bite. There are a couple of "nevers" with pizza stones, though:

- Never put a cold stone in a hot oven
- Never put a hot stone in cold water
- Never use soap or any kind of detergent to clean it; just water and scraping
- Never think you can just pick up a hot pizza stone with an oven mitt. It's way too hot, and some of 'em are so heavy, you might end up dropping it on your oven door, and then you have a mess. Best just to leave the stone in the oven all the time.
- Never let your wife talk you into buying an expensive one because a stone is a stone is a stone. Even the cheaper ones will work just fine. And besides, when your wife cooks something goofy on it, like a caramel bread, and burns it into the stone, it's ruined and you have to go buy a new one anyway.

Step 2 • Shaping the Dough

Pizzas should be baked one at a time, so only form the dough when you are ready to cook it. You can roll out the dough with a pin, or toss it in the air, just like a Neapolitan pizza maker.

After the dough is shaped, you'll need to put it down somewhere, put the toppings on it, then slide it into the oven without the pizza falling apart. Some people use a fancy wooden baker's paddle (also called a pizza peel), but you can just as easily use the back of a large baking sheet. Or, you can place the rolled dough onto large sheets of parchment paper. Whatever you're going to use to slide the pizza into the oven, sprinkle that surface with cornmeal. The cornmeal acts like little wheels and will allow your pizzas to slide right onto the stone safely.

To roll out the dough, flatten the ball into a disk on a lightly floured work surface. Dust the top of the dough with flour, and roll it into a 12-inch round.

If you want to try your hand at tossing the dough, dip both sides of your hands in flour, even your knuckles (because that's where the pizza dough will rest). Lift out a dough ball, and place it on a floured surface. Press the dough into a flat disk about 1/2 inch thick and 5 inches wide. Sprinkle more flour on top of the dough, and now gently pick it up. Make a fist, and place the dough circle on your fist. Now make your other hand into a fist and slide it up next to the first fist, to help pull out the dough. Gently bounce the dough on your knuckles to spread it out. Give it a few tiny tosses, *moving your hands apart to propel the dough into a spin.* (If the dough keeps springing back and refusing to expand, set it down and let it rest for 10 minutes; then try again.) Keep tossing and spinning the dough until it is about 10 inches across.

Transfer the round of dough to a cornmeal-dusted paddle, baking sheet, or sheet of parchment paper. If the round loses its shape, just reshape it on the paddle. Repeat with the remaining dough.

Step 3 • Topping Your Pizza

The key to a great Italian pizza is to go light on the toppings. You don't want to overload your precious crust, or pile ingredients on it that will break down and make a soggy mess. You should spread no more than 1/3 cup of sauce over the dough (you should be able to see the crust through it in places). Vegetables can give off lots of juices that will make your pizza soggy, so give them a quick sauté first so most of their moisture is evaporated before using as a topping. When you add the ingredients to the top, leave a 3/4-inch-wide border around the perimeter of the dough.

Teresa's T·I·P

If your dough isn't playing nice, and is instead sticking to your hands and refusing to stay in a ball, put the dough in time-out.

Leave the dough on the floured surface, and place your empty bowl upside down on top of it. Now walk away and leave it to think about what it did wrong for three to five minutes. When you come back, you'll find the dough to be a lot better behaved.

This also works well with kids (minus the bowl thing). Now if only it worked for husbands or boyfriends, right? Or mothers-in-law. Or ex-prostitutes who live around the corner . . .

Old World Pizza

Step 4 • *Baking Your Pizza*

Slide your pizza onto the pizza stone in your oven (or, if you're not using a stone, place the baking sheet with the pizza on it directly into the oven). Bake it for 8 to 10 minutes, until the crust is golden brown and slightly blistered. Now take it out, and let it sit for 3 minutes on your counter to set. Now cut and enjoy the best pizza of your life!

OLD WORLD PIZZA DOUGH

MAKES 6 PIZZA DOUGH
BALLS, ENOUGH FOR
SIX 10-INCH PIZZAS

Now that you know what to do with them, I can give you my secret ingredients for the best pizza crust this side of the moon.

¹/₄ cup extra virgin olive oil, plus more for rising

1 ¹/₄ teaspoons instant (bread machine) yeast

4 ¹/₂ cups bread flour, as needed

1 ¹/₂ teaspoons salt

1. To make the dough by hand, combine 1 ³/₄ cups cold water, the oil, and the yeast in a large bowl. Stir in 1 cup of the flour and the salt. Gradually stir in enough of the remaining flour to make a sticky dough that is too stiff to stir. Turn the dough out onto a well-floured work surface. Knead, adding more flour as necessary, until the dough is smooth and elastic (this means that when you stretch the dough a couple of inches in opposite directions, it snaps back into shape), about 5 minutes. The dough will remain slightly sticky, so don't overdo it with the flour.

To make the dough in a heavy-duty standing mixer, combine 1 ³/₄ cups cold water, the oil, and the yeast in the work bowl. Attach the bowl to the mixer and affix the paddle attachment. With the machine on low speed,

continues on page 142

*Pizza dough does
take a bit of time
and tender loving
care—and two
hours to rise—so I
usually make a big
batch and freeze
the extra dough so
I have it on hand
for a quick meal
another day.*

add 1 cup of the flour and the salt. Gradually add enough of the flour to make a stiff, sticky dough that clears the sides of the bowl. Switch to the dough hook. Knead on medium-low speed, adding more flour if necessary, until the dough is smooth and elastic, about 5 minutes. Turn the dough out onto a lightly floured work surface and knead briefly.

2. Cut the dough into 6 equal pieces and form each into a ball. Pour a couple of tablespoons of the oil into a 13 × 9-inch baking dish. Place each ball into the dish, turn to completely coat with oil, and turn smooth side up in the dish, leaving space between the balls. Cover tightly with plastic wrap. Refrigerate the covered dough for at least 12 hours and up to 3 days. (The dough can be frozen, each ball in its own small plastic freezer bag, for up to 3 months. Defrost in the refrigerator for at least 12 hours before using.) If you are really in a hurry, let the covered dough stand at room temperature until the balls double in size, about 1 1/2 hours, and skip the next step.

3. About 3 hours before baking, pour a few tablespoons of oil in a clean bowl. One at a time, coat each ball in fresh oil, and return to the baking dish, smooth side up. Cover again with plastic wrap and let stand at room temperature until doubled in size, about 2 hours. If the dough is really chilled from the refrigerator, it could take a little longer.

4. One at a time, drop each ball onto a lightly floured work surface, and press on the dough to deflate it. Shape into a ball again, return to the dish, cover, and let stand at room temperature to relax for 20 minutes. The dough is now ready to become pizza!

Our Family's Favorite Pizzas

I love just adding some marinara sauce, fresh mozzarella, and fresh parsley to my homemade pizzas, but here are a few other faves in our house.

PIZZA MARGHERITA

MAKES ONE
10-INCH PIZZA

This is a classic Italian pizza named after Queen Margherita of Italy because it was her favorite. It's a simple, three-ingredient pizza that has all the colors of the Italian flag: red, white, and green.

Cornmeal, for the paddle

Bread flour, for shaping the dough

1 ball Old World Pizza Dough (page 141)

1 large plum tomato, seeded and cut into 1/2-inch dice

2 ounces sliced fresh mozzarella, cut into 1-inch strips

1 teaspoon extra virgin olive oil

3 large fresh basil leaves, chopped

1. At least 30 minutes before baking, place a baking stone on the lowest rack of the oven, and preheat the oven to 475°F.

2. Sprinkle a wooden baker's paddle with cornmeal. Following the directions on page 138, shape the dough into a 10-inch round. Transfer to the paddle.

3. Top the dough with the tomato and mozzarella, leaving a 3/4-inch border. Drizzle with the oil.

4. Slide the pizza onto the baking stone. Bake until the crust is golden brown and slightly blistered, 8 to 10 minutes. Use the paddle to remove the pizza from the oven. Sprinkle with the basil. Let stand 3 minutes, then cut and serve hot.

PIZZA GIUDICE

This is how we do the queen's pizza in the Giudice kitchen.

**MAKES ONE
10-INCH PIZZA**

Cornmeal, for the paddle

Bread flour, for shaping the dough

1 ball Old World Pizza Dough (page 141)

1 large ripe plum tomato, seeded and cut into $\frac{1}{2}$-inch dice

1 garlic clove, minced

2 teaspoons extra virgin olive oil

$\frac{1}{4}$ cup freshly grated Pecorino Romano

1 tablespoon finely chopped fresh parsley

1. At least 30 minutes before baking, place a baking stone on the lowest rack of the oven, and preheat the oven to 475°F.

2. Sprinkle a wooden baker's paddle with cornmeal. Following the directions on page 138, shape the dough into a 10-inch round. Transfer to the paddle.

3. Mix the diced tomato, garlic, and oil together in a small bowl (yes, I do this with my hands). Scatter over the dough, then sprinkle with the Romano, leaving a $\frac{3}{4}$-inch border.

4. Slide the pizza onto the baking stone. Bake until the crust is golden brown and slightly blistered, 8 to 10 minutes. Use the paddle to remove the pizza from the oven. Sprinkle with the parsley. Let stand 3 minutes, then cut and serve hot.

PIZZA WITH ANCHOVIES AND GARLIC

MAKES ONE

10-INCH PIZZA

I love-love-love anchovies, especially on a pizza!

Cornmeal, for the paddle

Bread flour, for shaping the dough

1 ball Old World Pizza Dough (page 141)

**One 2-ounce tin flat anchovy fillets in olive oil,
   drained and minced**

2 tablespoons extra virgin olive oil

2 garlic cloves, minced

1. At least 30 minutes before baking, place a baking stone on the lowest rack of the oven, and preheat the oven to 475°F.

2. Sprinkle a wooden baker's paddle with cornmeal. Following the directions on page 138, shape the dough into a 10-inch round. Transfer to the paddle.

3. Mix the anchovies, oil, and garlic together in a small bowl. Spread over the dough, leaving a ³/4-inch border.

4. Slide the pizza onto the baking stone. Bake until the crust is golden brown and slightly blistered, 8 to 10 minutes. Use the paddle to remove the pizza from the oven. Let stand 3 minutes, then cut and serve hot.

PIZZA NAPOLETANA

This is a well-known pizza in Naples, Italy, and it's one of my favorites.

MAKES ONE
10-INCH PIZZA

Cornmeal, for the paddle

Bread flour, for shaping the dough

1 ball Old World Pizza Dough (page 141)

1/3 cup Milania's Marinara Sauce (page 119)

3 drained anchovy fillets, coarsely chopped

1 tablespoon drained capers

2 ounces sliced fresh mozzarella, cut into 1-inch strips

1 teaspoon dried oregano

2 teaspoons extra virgin olive oil

1. At least 30 minutes before baking, place a baking stone on the lowest rack of the oven, and preheat the oven to 475°F.

2. Sprinkle a wooden baker's paddle with cornmeal. Following the directions on page 138, shape the dough into a 10-inch round. Transfer to the paddle.

3. Spread the marinara sauce over the dough, leaving a 3/4-inch border. The rest is like a school art project: dot the anchovies and capers all over the pizza, making a pretty design if you'd like. Sprinkle with the cheese, then the oregano. Drizzle with the oil.

4. Slide the pizza onto the baking stone. Bake until the crust is golden brown and slightly blistered, 8 to 10 minutes. Use the paddle to remove the pizza from the oven. Let stand 3 minutes, then cut and serve hot.

PIZZA AL PROSCIUTTO

This is the Italian version of a Hawaiian pizza, only with beautiful prosciutto instead of just ham, and without warm, soggy pineapple.

Cornmeal, for the paddle

Bread flour, for shaping the dough

1 ball Old World Pizza Dough (page 141)

1/3 cup Milania's Marinara Sauce (page 119)

2 ounces thinly sliced prosciutto, cut into 1-inch pieces

2 ounces sliced fresh mozzarella, cut into 1-inch strips

1 teaspoon extra virgin olive oil

1. At least 30 minutes before baking, place a baking stone on the lowest rack of the oven, and preheat the oven to 475°F.

2. Sprinkle a wooden baker's paddle with cornmeal. Following the directions on page 138, shape the dough into a 10-inch round. Transfer to the paddle.

3. Spread the marinara sauce over the dough, leaving a 3/4-inch border. Top with the prosciutto, then the cheese. Drizzle with the oil.

4. Slide the pizza onto the baking stone. Bake until the crust is golden brown and slightly blistered, 8 to 10 minutes. Use the paddle to remove the pizza from the oven. Let stand 3 minutes, then cut and serve hot.

Pizza with Italian Sausage

MAKES ONE

10-INCH PIZZA

Of course, sausage isn't the leanest meat, but if you're going to have it on a pizza (as a treat, not an everyday thing), at least do it up right, and make it healthier with the olive oil. You can also use turkey sausage, or do like Joe does, and mix the turkey sausage with the real stuff.

Cornmeal, for the paddle

Bread flour, for shaping the dough

1 ball Old World Pizza Dough (page 141)

2 teaspoons extra virgin olive oil

2 links (4 ounces) sweet or hot Italian sausage, casings removed

1 medium onion, cut into ⅛-inch half-moons

½ red bell pepper, cored, seeded, and cut into ⅛-inch half-moons

1. At least 30 minutes before baking, place a baking stone on the lowest rack of the oven, and preheat the oven to 475°F.

2. Sprinkle a wooden baker's paddle with cornmeal. Following the directions on page 138, shape the dough into a 10-inch round. Transfer to the paddle.

3. Heat the oil in a medium skillet over medium-high heat. Add the sausage and cook, breaking up the meat with the side of a spoon, until lightly browned, about 5 minutes. Using a slotted spoon, transfer the sausage to a bowl, leaving the fat in the pan. Add the onion and bell pepper and cook, stirring occasionally, until limp, about 3 minutes. Using the slotted spoon, transfer to the bowl. Let cool.

4. Scatter the sausage and vegetables over the dough, leaving a ¾-inch border. Slide the pizza onto the baking stone. Bake until the crust is golden brown and slightly blistered, 8 to 10 minutes. Use the paddle to remove the pizza from the oven. Let stand 3 minutes, then cut and serve hot.

9 Scratching It Up in the Kitchen

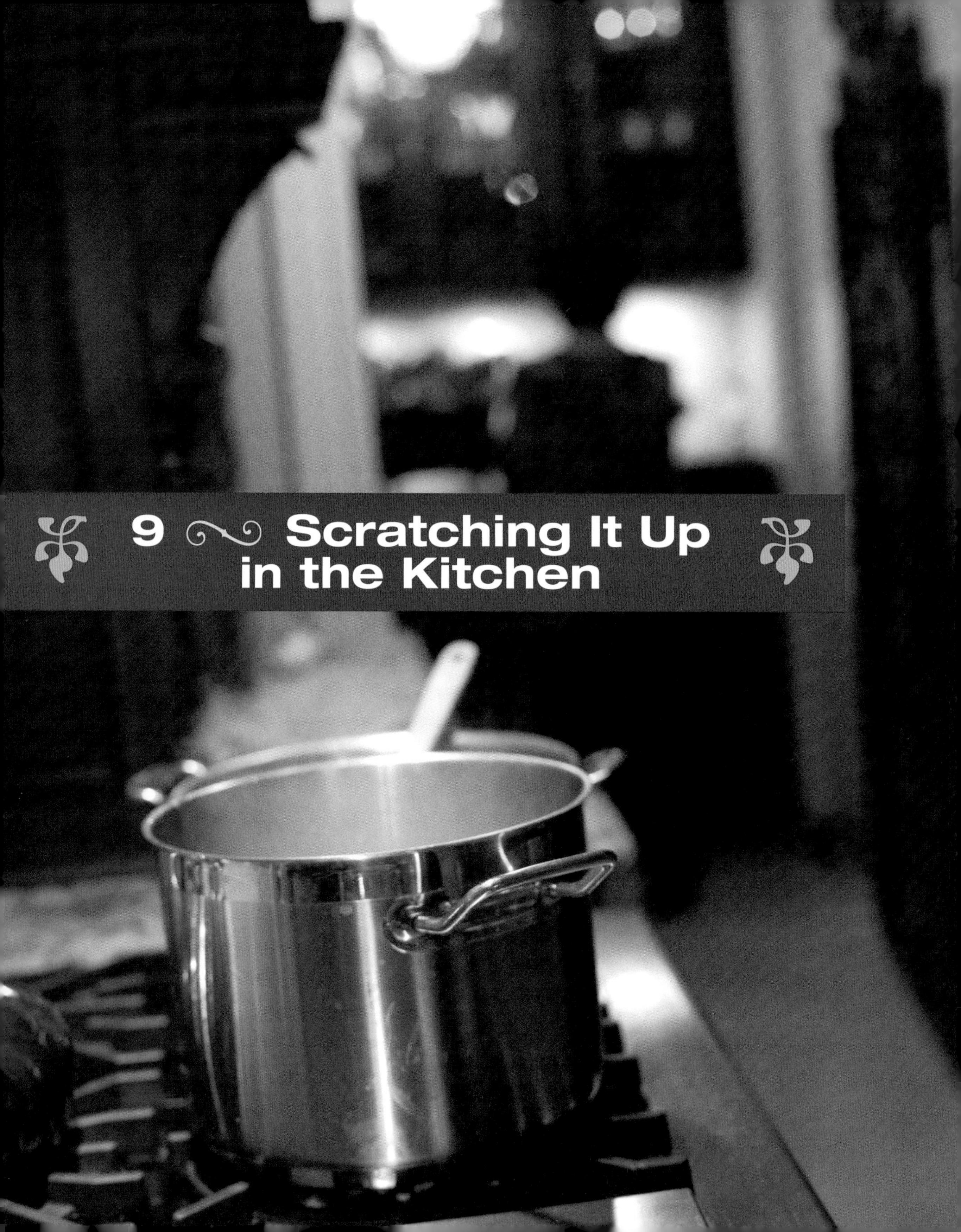

I already taught you how to make amazing homemade sauces and perfect pizza from scratch. Now that you're all the way to Chapter 9, I think it's time to graduate. You are no longer a little kitchen bitch. You are ready for the big time: canning your own tomatoes. Conquer this and you have my full permission to call yourself a hot Italian mamma!

At the end of every August, Italians around the world prepare for their annual tomato canning ritual. And when I say "prepare," I mean, like, make a hundred freakin' jars of the stuff! Enough to last your family a full year.

There's a million ways to do it, but this is my way, and, of course, it's the best. In my family, we call it a celebration, rather than a chore, because sweating over a hot stove for hours making a year's worth of sauce is no walk in the park; but if you pour yourself a nice glass of wine, invite your friends over, and put on some music, you can enjoy this delicious day!

Tomatoes. Period.

Remember, both my parents and my in-laws, as well as Joe, actually, were all born in Italy. And in Italy, we have tons of legends and stories and special ways of doing things. One of those "special ways" actually has to do with tomato canning and having your period.

In Italy, it's widely believed that if a woman is menstruating, she can't be around the fresh tomatoes or they will all spoil. I know so many people in the old country who have stories about this, and my dad swears it's true. I think it's funny, but since I was pregnant, there obviously wasn't a problem this year.

My dad, however, had to take a poll. He actually asked our babysitter if it was her time of month! *Madonna mia!*

I'm not saying I believe it, but your Italian grandmother was right about the peels of potatoes and the crust of bread being the most nutritious parts . . .

The Tomato Canning Celebration

My ma always comes over, and me and the girls have our little tomato-sauce party. This year was our biggest production ever because my entire family was there, including my in-laws, to help out because I was two weeks away from having my baby Audriana. And it was the first day Bravo decided to film us for Season Two of *The Real Housewives of New Jersey*, so my kitchen was full of canning equipment and camera guys, extra lights, and total craziness.

Thank goodness for my girls! No matter what chaos is going on around us, they just make me smile. Gia tied a bandanna around her head and she looked just like a little Italian country girl. She was so serious with the tomatoes. My mother-in-law told her she'd be a very good wife someday, and asked what kind of guy she wanted to marry. She's so cute, she said, "I'm too young to worry about who I'm going to marry!" Then she changed her mind and said an Italian man like her daddy. (More people quote Gia to me from Season One than anyone else. The favorite seems to be from when I put lip gloss on Gia for her dance recital, and she told everyone: "My mom did it!")

It was a really great day—it always is—full of family and laughter and tomato juice everywhere. You should definitely get your friends or family together and try it just once. Just promise me that you'll all tie bandannas around your heads and quote Gia no fewer than thirty times.

The Tools of the Trade

If you don't have them on hand, you're going to need a few items, but they aren't expensive, you can use them year after year, and the money you'll save (and the hearts you'll win) making your own sauce will be well worth it!

Boiling Water Canner

A boiling water canner is a huge, deep pot with a tight lid and a rack that sits on the bottom inside (to keep the jars from touching the bottom of the pot and touching each other). You can find them at grocery stores or regular retailers, and, of course, on the Internet. They cost anywhere from thirty to ninety dollars, depending on how fancy you want the extras: some have racks that lift in and out of the water, some have silicone handles that don't get hot, some have see-through glass lids. Get what you like.

If you don't want to buy a boiling water canner, you can just use a really deep saucepan (it has to be deep enough to cover your jars with one to two inches of water and still have room for all the boiling) and place a circular cake rack on the bottom.

A twenty-one-quart pot—the average size for canning—will hold seven quart jars.

The Jars

Get good thick jars made to withstand the heat of boiling. You can't just reuse an old mayonnaise jar or something. They're called canning jars, but also Mason jars, Kerr jars, or Ball jars, after the manufacturers who made them.

They come in many different sizes, with regular-sized openings or wide mouth (I like the wide-mouthed ones; they're less messy). They cost anywhere from fifty cents to a dollar apiece, and you can reuse them over and over.

The Jar Lids

Sometimes the jars come with lids; sometimes you have to buy them separately. A jar lid has two parts: the dome lid (the flat part with the rubbery seal on the inside) and the canning band (the screw-ring part). The dome lid sits directly on the top of the glass jar. The canning band just holds it in place while you boil the jar.

You can reuse the screw rings every year, but you have to buy new dome lids because of bacteria and stuff.

Canning Tools

You're also going to need a jar lifter because the glass jars will be hot (unless you have a rack that lifts out nicely, and then you can use an oven mitt). Save yourself the mess and get a canning funnel.

You don't need a magnetic lid lifter, bubble remover, headspace gauge, or any of that other crap. Save your money; use a thin plastic spatula.

Food/Vegetable Strainer

This isn't like a colander that you put in your sink to drain the water out of pasta. A food strainer is a machine that clamps to your kitchen counter and separates the skin and seeds from the cooked tomato pulp. It sort of looks like a meat grinder, but it's for vegetables. I have a hand-crank type, and it works well. There are also electric ones and ones that come as attachments to your kitchen mixer.

If you're only making a couple jars (and why go through all that trouble, really?), you can get by without a strainer. You can blanch and peel the toma-

If you can believe it, many people think tomatoes are an aphrodisiac. I can kind of see why—they're all red and moist and whatnot.

The Aztecs called them *tomatl*, or "the swelling fruit." In France, they were called *pommes d'amour*, or "love apples." But no one believes in their sexual power like the Italians. In fact, at one time the Catholic Church actually banned eating ripe tomatoes in public because it was considered a "lewd and lascivious act."

Where I come from, if you call a girl a "tomato," it's a compliment; means she's good-lookin'. I don't know if tomatoes are exactly the secret to all of mine and Teresa's kids, but she is definitely one hot tomato in my book!

toes yourself. But when you're making 160 jars, you're gonna want this little machine. It's only like forty dollars and is well, well worth it!

The Tomatoes

Now that we've got the tools, we need the food!

Start with a trip to your local farmer's market. Even if you've never gone at the end of August before, the vendors there are ready for the Italian sauce makers. The tomatoes are piled up, rich and juicy, ripe and beautiful, ready to be taken home. You won't have to sift through, squeezing and sorting out the crappy ones, like you do at the supermarket.

You only want to use big plum tomatoes: the long-looking, oval-shaped ones. Plum tomatoes are also called processing or paste tomatoes because they are the best for making sauces. They are harder than round tomatoes, and have way fewer seeds. They also handle really well.

There are a couple different varieties of plum tomatoes: Roma VF, San Marzano, Ropreco Paste, and Big Mama, to name a few. Whatever your local market has will work great. Just tell them you're making tomato sauce, and they'll take care of you.

My family of six goes through about 160 jars in a year. You can get around sixteen jars per bushel of tomatoes, so I usually buy ten bushels. Do your own math and buy what you need.

While you're at the market, also pick up some fresh basil, and a bunch of flowers to make yourself feel good. You deserve it for what you're about to do!

Ten Easy Steps

Now, for all of my bitching about the hot kitchen and having to fill millions of jars, it's really easy, really worth it, and it will save you tons of money and time throughout the year. It might look complicated at first (I know boiling a jar for the first time can be scary), but there are just ten super-easy steps. Stick with me and you'll have hungry guys eating out of the palm of your hand in no time!

Step 1 • Wash the Jars and Lids

Wash them in hot, soapy water. Easy, right?

Step 2 • Sanitize the Jars

Fill your boiling water canner (the big pot) halfway with water, and then place your jars (no lids) on the rack inside. Add more water until the jars are covered, and boil over medium-high heat for 10 minutes. Take the jars out and let them dry, but don't place them anywhere they might get too cold. You'll use that water again in Step 8 to seal the jars.

Step 3 • Wash the Tomatoes

Wash all of your tomatoes real nice. Take off the stems and remove any bad spots.

Ten Easy Steps!

Step 4 • Boil the Tomatoes

Fill a second pot (6 to 8 quarts) with water. Bring it to a boil over high heat. Add your tomatoes and boil them until the skins just start to crack.

Step 5 • Strain the Tomatoes

Remove the tomatoes from the boiling water and run them under cold water. You can either feed them into the vegetable strainer now, which will remove the skin and seeds with a couple turns of the crank, or use ice water and a knife to skin and cut the tomatoes and remove the seeds. Gather all of your pulp into a big bowl.

Step 6 • Stuff Your Jars

Take the tomato pulp and scoop it into your jars (this is where the funnel comes in handy). And for goodness sake, use a big spoon to scoop the pulp. If my mother comes in and sees you trying to pour sauce right out of the bowl into that tiny funnel, there'll be hell to pay! Fill the jars, but leave ½ inch of room at the top. (They call this the "headspace.")

Step 7 • Really Stuff Your Jars

Stick a thin spatula into the jar and push the tomatoes toward the center to remove any air bubbles. Do this around the entire jar three or four times. Add some more tomato if you need to and pack it down again. Now stick a big piece of basil into the jar and close it up. Wipe the edges of the jar to remove any spillage, and make sure the dome lid is on the very center with a good grip on the jar. Screw the canning band onto the jar until it won't move anymore, but not too tight.

Step 8 • Processing (Boiling) the Jars

Bring the water in your boiling water canner to a simmer (about 180°F), and carefully add your jars (keep them upright and be careful not to tip them!). Make sure the jars are covered with 1 or 2 inches of water. Cover the canner with its lid and bring the whole thing to a rolling boil over medium-high heat. Keep the jars in the steady boil for 20 minutes.

Step 9 • Removing the Jars

Using the lifting rack or a special jar lifter, remove the jars one at a time from the water and place them on a towel on your counter. The jars are damn hot, so be careful! And try to keep them as straight as possible; no tipping. Leave the jars exactly where they are for 12 hours to cool. Don't screw with the lids or shake them around or anything. Leave them be.

Step 10 • Test, Store, Finito!

After the jars have cooled, test each one to make sure it has a solid seal. The dome lids should be slightly concave, sucked into the middle of the jar just a bit. When you push on them, they shouldn't budge. Unscrew the band and gently pull on the lid. If it stays on, you've got a good seal. If it pops off, your jar didn't seal. It doesn't mean your sauce is wasted; you just can't store that jar. Pop it in the fridge and use it in the next couple of days.

Some people take the bands off and store the jars with just the lids, but that looks a little off to me. I like the big thick screwy lid. Just make sure you wipe the edges of the jar and remove any water, so the band won't rust and make it a chore to open later.

That's it! You can now store your jars of tomato sauce (or give them as gifts to the Italian-mamma-bes in your town) for up to a year. A cool, dark place is best; your regular pantry will do just fine.

Everything about Italy is art-art-art: from the gorgeous paintings to the beautiful buildings to the amazing fashion designers . . . even flirting is an art form. (Italian men, *ah marone*!) There is also an art to eating in Italy—a certain way of serving, of entertaining, even of chewing your food that makes everything a little slower, a little sexier, and a lot healthier.

The Slow Food Movement

Everything about America is fast: fast food, fast cars, fast women (well, some of them, anyway). Things are so fast now the baby comes before the wedding, and the engagement comes before anyone's even met the family. We talk fast, we drink fast, I think we even have sex too fast (too soon, with too many people, and then not long enough each time . . . but that's another book).

Every country knows America is fast, and they love the energy they find when they visit us here, but not every country wants to do things as fast as we do. In 1986, when McDonald's wanted to open their first restaurant in

Italy, the company chose a really sacred place to the Italians: in Rome right next to the *Piazza di Spagna*, the Spanish Steps. It's one thing to take American fast food to Italy, but to drop it in such a special place did not make people happy. A guy named Carlo Petrini led a protest of locals all holding bowls of penne. (McDonald's went ahead and opened their restaurant there, and it was their largest franchise in the world at the time. Gross!)

It's not that McDonald's is the cause of all the unhealthy eating, but with 31,000 restaurants in 119 countries (they're even putting one in the Louvre museum in Paris!), unhealthy fast-food options are becoming the only option in a lot of places. There's a fast-food restaurant on every corner in cities, but it can be hard to find healthy alternatives. Today, none of us has enough time or enough money, so a 99-cent meal seems like a deal. But in the long run, it's killing us.

Petrini started an international organization called Slow Food to remind everyone about the benefits of slowing down when we eat. (Their logo is so cute; it's a little gold snail!) Slow Food now has more than 100,000 members in 132 countries (so he beat McDonald's at something!), and many restaurants now have the Slow Food snail outside their door to let you know they support locally grown food, local cuisine, and the enjoyment of eating it.

I'm all over this cause. I think it's great. There is nothing more aggravating than taking your family out to eat and feeling rushed. No sir! I want to sit and enjoy being out of my house and eating delicious food cooked by someone else for a change.

I used to work with a girl named Kim who was always running around as if her hair was on fire. She had three kids and was stick thin (I didn't have any kids yet) and she said her secret was that she "never had time to eat." She wouldn't fix herself dinner, she'd just eat the leftovers on her kids' plates and that kept her thin. I'm all for fitting into those skinny jeans, but not that way. That's just bad, bad, bad! And sad!

I know a lot of women, though, who eat like this. Whether it's a crazy house full of kids at dinnertime, or working women eating their lunch while running between meetings. Eating isn't supposed to be a job, it's supposed to be a joy.

The family dinner is an important tradition to keep alive with the next generation. When I was a kid, my dad got home from work every night at 5:30 p.m., and dinner was waiting for him on the table. If we kids weren't at the dinner table when he walked in the door, we'd get our asses kicked. There was just no excuse. It was about respect.

We all pitched in for dinner. My mom would even make me clean the kitchen floors before I could go out and play.

Today, life is so much busier and we got people calling us on our cell phones at all hours and we're expected to be on call for everyone. But you gotta lay down the law. It's your life. Not your boss's life. Whether you got a house full of munchkins like I do, or your life is quieter, don't let anyone interrupt you when you're eating.

When he was interviewed by *Time* magazine in 2004, Petrini explained his belief that we should "surely, slowly, fully and without excess, enjoy the pleasures of the senses." Amen to that!

The Benefits of Slowing Down

Even the doctors and nutritionists are jumping on this "slow down" thing. It's good for your health because it stops you from overeating. It takes fifteen to twenty minutes for your stomach to let your brain know that you've eaten something. If you scarf down too much food too fast, your body will never have to chance to tell you it's already full.

Eating slowly and enjoying your food can also help boost your metabolism, which is great because a fast metabolism is your skinny jeans' friend. It seems like the opposite: if you run around, even eating fast, you're burning calories, and if you sit still to eat slowly, your body will slow down, so you might as well grab and go, right? Not according to the brown trout.

In 2000, the Institute of Biomedical and Life Sciences at the University of Glasgow did this huge experiment with fish and found that when the fish were stressed—which is what you are when you're running around like a maniac—the stress hormones they released slowed their metabolism down. When they were calm, they had happy hormones and a nice, fast metabolism. It's true for humans, too. You might lose weight when you're super stressed, but it's a temporary, unhealthy weight loss. Our goal is a happy life in which we can eat delicious food and still look fabulous!

Italian Dinner, Family Style

In Italy, eating is traditionally a long, amazing process enjoyed with your friends and family. There's no grabbing food as you run out the door. When I was growing up, we ate dinner as a family every night, and we still do. I think it's one of the reasons my kids know how to sit still at a restaurant and behave, because they've learned that eating isn't bounce-off-the-walls time (that's what they do with their other twenty-two hours a day).

No matter what day of the week it is, special occasion or not, there is a ritual to the Italian dinner. Dinner usually takes around two hours and wine or mineral water is served throughout the meal. The dishes served in order are:

- *Aperitivo*
  (before-dinner drink)

- *L'antipasto*
  (bread, cheese, or veggie appetizers, served during the *aperitivo*)

- *La Prima Piatta*
  (a small pasta dish)

- *La Seconda Piatta*
  (the main meat course served with a vegetable or salad)

- *Il Dolce e Caffè*
  (dessert and coffee)

The Hostess with the Most-est

Part of planning a great meal is being a great hostess, and that starts with the guest list. You don't have to invite everybody in your neighborhood over at one time. Make sure you invite people who all get along (or you might find yourself with a flipped table or two).

As the hostess, make sure you mingle and talk to everyone. It's your job to make everyone feel comfortable and relaxed.

An Italian dinner is a time for laughing.

Bad topics: politics, money, tell-all books written by your guest's ex-husband.

Good topics: fashion, children, friends, the old days, sex.

It seems like a lot of food, but remember, the portions are smaller and we take our time eating it.

Today, most Italians reserve Sunday for their traditional dinner, and have a shortened version for other days. We often also skip the pasta course (it's usually more of a lunch meal), or the pasta is incorporated into the main dish. I'm going to teach you how to master each stage of the Italian dinner so you can make every meal a feast. If you're not entertaining a big crowd, even if you're eating alone, I still want to encourage you to savor each bite, eat slowly, and enjoy the divine process.

Delicious Drinks

Since the Roman times, Italians have begun their eating rituals with a mini cocktail hour. The idea of a before-dinner drink is not only to help your guests relax and unwind from a long day, but also to help open up your digestive system and get your stomach ready for eating. (Don't believe me? The Italian word *aperitivo* comes from the Latin *aperire*, which means "to open up.")

This is not a time to get trashed, or to see how many beers you can chug. You don't want to ruin your appetite, you want to enhance it. For this part of your meal, you want everyone walking around, sipping their drinks and sampling the appetizers. Make sure you've got on some good music, and your party will come to life!

Good drinks to have on hand are Campari, Prosecco, vodka, vermouth, sodas, and fruit juices (we love to mix alcohol with fruit juices!). While beer is considered tacky, wine is OK, and sparkling wine like Spumante is even better.

BELLISSIMO BELLINIS

MAKES 6 DRINKS

Teresa's T·I·P

The easiest way to peel fresh peaches? Drop them into a saucepan of boiling water, and cook for 30 seconds. Using a slotted spoon, transfer them to a bowl of ice water. Let stand a minute or so, then drain and peel.

My favorite, favorite drink is the Bellini: a mix of sparkling Italian wine and peaches. (I've been told I get funnier with each Bellini, but who doesn't?)

This is the way they make it in Venice: with fresh white peaches and ripe raspberries. If fresh white peaches aren't in season, you can use regular or thawed frozen peaches, but I've even seen white peach puree online—well worth sticking in your freezer!

2 ripe white peaches, peeled, pitted, and coarsely chopped

¼ cup fresh or thawed frozen raspberries (frozen can be used, but should be thawed first)

One 750-ml bottle Italian sparking wine, such as Prosecco or Spumante, chilled

1. Puree the peaches in a blender. You should have ½ cup of peach puree. Pour into a small bowl. Rinse out the blender.

2. Puree the raspberries in the blender. Strain the raspberries through a wire sieve to remove the seeds. You should have at least 2 tablespoons of raspberry puree. Pour into a small bowl. If you have the time, cover each bowl of puree and refrigerate them so they are really chilled.

3. For each serving, spoon a heaping tablespoon of peach puree into the bottom of a Champagne flute. Top with about 1 teaspoon of the raspberry puree. Slowly fill the glass with the sparkling wine. To keep the foaming at a minimum, fill the glass halfway, let the fizzing subside, then finish with a second pour. Serve immediately.

LAZY BELLINIS

MAKES 6 BEVERAGES

You might not always have fresh peaches on hand, so here's a recipe for Lazy Bellinis (the kind they'll probably give you in a bar).

¾ cup peach schnapps, chilled

One 750-ml bottle sparkling Italian wine, such as Prosecco or Spumante, chilled

For each serving, pour 2 tablespoons of schnapps into a Champagne flute. Slowly fill the glass with the sparkling wine, letting the foaming subside before adding more sparkling wine. Serve immediately.

"Skinny" Cocktails

Everyone would love to be able to enjoy their favorite hard alcoholic cocktail with fewer calories. Sadly, there are only two ways to do this.

1 • Compromise on the quality of the nonalcoholic extras; like use a "diet" orange drink instead of orange juice. But that's full of chemicals rather than just fruit.

2 • Lie about it • I'm sort of kidding, but it really doesn't matter what you do. You can't magically erase calories in alcohol, no matter what you call your cocktail. A margarita is a margarita is a margarita.

HOMEMADE LIMONCELLO

MAKES 48
2-OUNCE SERVINGS

Another classic Italian drink is limoncello, a lemon-flavored alcohol. Of course, you can buy bottled limoncello, but it's so much more fun to make it from scratch. You do need a full thirty to sixty days for curing, but it's well worth it!

16 lemons

Two 750-ml bottles 100-proof vodka

4 cups sugar

1. Wash the lemons thoroughly. Using a vegetable peeler, remove the yellow zest of the lemons in strips. Do not dig into the white pith underneath the zest, as it is very bitter. (You're done with the lemons now, so save them for something that uses lots of lemon juice.)

2. Transfer 1 bottle of vodka to a large, 1-gallon glass jar with a lid (such as a glass cookie jar, available inexpensively at housewares stores). Add the lemon zest, cover, and store in a cool, dark place for 15 to 30 days.

3. After this initial steeping period, bring 5 cups water and the sugar to a boil in a medium saucepan over high heat, stirring to dissolve the sugar. Boil, stirring occasionally, until slightly thickened, about 5 minutes. Cool completely.

4. Pour the syrup into the jar. Add the remaining bottle of vodka. Cover again and let stand in a cool, dark place for 15 to 30 days more.

5. Strain the limoncello through a wire sieve to remove the zest. Pour the limoncello into attractive glass bottles. Store in the freezer until you are ready to use.

DINA'S VIRGIN MIMOSA

Next to a Bellini, a mimosa is my favorite drink (naturally, we make ours with Italian sparkling wine instead of Champagne). But sometimes you're out with a friend who doesn't like to drink a lot of alcohol (or can't for medical reasons or something), but she still wants to have fun. Drinking bottled water or Diet Coke when everyone else has something fizzy and fruity is not fun.

Of course, you can buy San Pellegrino Limonatas at the grocery store, but those have a lemony taste, and when you're in a bar, anyone can mix up the Dina Virgin for you!

1/4 cup fresh orange juice, strained to remove pulp

1/2 cup sparkling water, preferably San Pellegrino

Pour orange juice into a Champagne flute. Fill up the glass with San Pellegrino.

Dina

Dina is one of my best friends. I've known her for fifteen years; I actually met her when she was pregnant with Lexie. She loves to hang out at lounges with me and Jacqueline, but she's not a big drinker. I created this virgin mimosa for her, so she could get just as crazy as we do with our Champagne glasses and bubbles. (Only she's funny because she's naturally funny, not because she's had one too many!)

Amazing Appetizers

Fruit, olives, cheese, meats, and vegetables are the most common Italian appetizers, along with bruschetta, grissini, and any amazing topping you can pour, scoop, or smush onto them. The best thing about Italian breads for appetizers is that they are flat, thin, and crispy, have lots of air holes, and don't have too many carbs (unlike, say, a big, soft bread bowl filled with dill dip you might find at an American party). Italian appetizers go anywhere from really simple (just get some grissini at the store, wrap the ends in prosciutto, and stand them in a pretty glass, and you've got one!) to stuffed, baked, and fabulous. Here are the antipastos I almost always serve at my house.

BRUSCHETTA CLASSICA

1 loaf wide, crusty Italian bread
   (not one with too many holes in the crumb),
   cut diagonally into twelve $1/2$-inch slices

3 tablespoons extra virgin olive oil

5 plum tomatoes, cored, seeded, and cut into $1/2$-inch dice

1 teaspoon balsamic vinegar

1 teaspoon dried oregano

1 garlic clove, minced

$1/2$ teaspoon salt

$1/4$ teaspoon freshly ground black pepper

1. Position a rack in the center of the oven and preheat the oven to 450°F.

2. Arrange the sliced bread on a large baking sheet. Brush with 2 table-spoons of the oil. Bake just until the bread starts to toast, about 5 minutes. Let cool.

3. Mix the tomatoes, remaining 1 tablespoon olive oil, vinegar, oregano, garlic, salt, and pepper in a bowl, taking care not to crush the tomatoes. Let stand at room temperature for about an hour for the flavors to blend.

4. Arrange the bread slices on a platter with the oiled side up. Top each slice with some of the tomato mixture and serve immediately. (If you prefer, serve the tomato mixture in a fancy bowl with a spoon, and allow your guests to top their own slices.)

BRUSCHETTA E PROSCIUTTO

MAKES 12 SERVINGS

1 loaf wide, crusty Italian bread
   (not one with too many holes in the crumb),
   cut diagonally into twelve $1/2$-inch slices

2 tablespoons extra virgin olive oil

1 garlic clove, minced

$1/8$ teaspoon freshly ground black pepper

4 ounces thinly sliced prosciutto, cut into 1-inch pieces

$1/4$ cup freshly grated Parmigiano-Reggiano

1 tablespoon chopped fresh parsley

1. Position a rack in the center of the oven and preheat the oven to 450°F.

2. Arrange the bread slices on a large baking sheet. Mix the oil, garlic, and pepper together in a small bowl. Spoon the garlic oil over the bread. Bake just until the bread starts to toast around the edges, about 3 minutes. Remove from the oven.

3. Arrange the prosciutto over the bread slices, then sprinkle with the Parmigiano-Reggiano. Return to the oven, and bake until the cheese is melted and begins to turn golden brown, about 4 minutes. Sprinkle with the parsley and serve hot.

CAPONATA BRUSCHETTA

MAKES 1 QUART
EGGPLANT MIXTURE,
16 SERVINGS

2 tablespoons extra virgin olive oil

1 medium onion, sliced

1 garlic clove, minced

1 large eggplant, trimmed and cut into strips
   about 3 inches long and 1/2 inch wide

3 ripe plum tomatoes, halved, seeded, and
   cut into 1/2-inch-wide strips

1/2 teaspoon dried oregano

1/2 teaspoon salt

1/4 teaspoon crushed hot red pepper

1/2 cup pitted and chopped kalamata olives

3 tablespoons drained capers

1 1/2 tablespoons balsamic vinegar

1 tablespoon chopped fresh parsley

1 loaf wide, crusty Italian bread
   (not one with too many holes in the crumb),
   cut diagonally into twelve 1/2-inch slices

1. Heat the oil in a large saucepan over medium heat. Add the onion and garlic and cook, stirring occasionally, until the onion softens, about 3 minutes. Add the eggplant, tomatoes, oregano, salt, and hot pepper and stir. Cover and reduce the heat to medium-low. Cook, stirring often, until very tender, about 20 minutes. Stir in the olives, capers, and vinegar.

2. Transfer to a serving bowl and sprinkle with the parsley. Serve hot or cooled, with the bread, allowing each guest to slather their bread with the eggplant mixture.

BALSAMIC GARLIC BITES

MAKES 8 SERVINGS

Even though they sound strong, boiled garlic bites do not have the same pungent taste as raw or fried garlic. The bites will come out smooth and creamy; you can spoon them over appetizers, smash them into a butter-like sauce for bread, serve them as part of an antipasti platter, or just eat them with a fork.

> 24 plump, firm garlic cloves, peeled so they remain intact
>
> 1 cup balsamic vinegar, as needed
>
> 1 tablespoon extra virgin olive oil

1. Place the garlic in a small saucepan, and add enough vinegar to cover. Bring to a boil, and reduce the heat to low. Cover and simmer until the garlic is tender, about 15 minutes.

2. Drain the garlic cloves (they will have dark purple spots on them from the vinegar), and let cool. Transfer to a small serving bowl. Drizzle the olive oil over the top and serve.

SALERNO STUFFED MUSHROOMS

MAKES 10 SERVINGS,
2 MUSHROOMS
PER PERSON

This recipe is straight from my mamma. She taught me how to make the best stuffed mushrooms. And now I'm teaching you.

> 20 large white mushrooms (at least 2 inches in diameter)
>
> 4 tablespoons olive oil
>
> 1 medium onion, finely chopped
>
> 1 garlic clove, minced

continues on page 184

¾ **cup dried plain bread crumbs**

½ **cup grated Pecorino Romano**

3 **tablespoons chopped fresh parsley**

¼ **teaspoon salt**

⅛ **teaspoon freshly ground black pepper**

1. Position a rack in the center of the oven, and preheat the oven to 350°F. Lightly oil a baking sheet.

2. Carefully wipe the mushrooms with a damp cloth or paper towel. Remove the stems, and set aside. With a small spoon, scoop out each mushroom cap so it looks like a little bowl, reserving the trimmings. Finely chop the stems and reserved trimmings.

3. Heat 2 tablespoons of the oil in a large nonstick skillet over medium heat. Add the onion and garlic and cook, stirring occasionally, until the onion is translucent, about 5 minutes. Add 1 tablespoon of the oil and the chopped mushroom mixture. Cook, stirring occasionally, until the mushrooms are tender, about 5 minutes. Transfer to a bowl and cool slightly.

4. Add the bread crumbs, cheese, 2 tablespoons of the parsley, the salt, and the pepper, and mix well. It should look like stuffing (because that's really what it is!).

5. Arrange the mushroom caps, cavity side up, on the baking sheet. Using a dinner spoon, fill each cap with the stuffing, using the spoon to shape the stuffing into a smooth mound. Drizzle the remaining 1 tablespoon of oil over the mushrooms.

6. Bake until the stuffing begins to brown, about 15 minutes. The mushrooms will shrink a little during baking. Transfer to a platter, sprinkle with the remaining parsley, and serve hot.

Divine Dinners

I love cooking so much that I make these dishes all the time. I make them at home, of course, but I also go to friends' houses, like Jacqueline's, and cook in their kitchens. They're easy, healthy, and delicious!

ONE-PAN OVEN-ROASTED CHICKEN FEAST

MAKES 6 SERVINGS

Teresa's
T·I·P

Don't have a meat pounder? No problem. You can use a rolling pin or, my favorite, an empty bottle of wine (just don't pound so hard that you break it or hurt yourself!).

FOR CHICKEN:

Six 6-ounce boneless and skinless chicken breasts

1/2 cup dry white wine

1/4 cup extra virgin olive oil

2 teaspoons dried oregano

2 garlic cloves, minced

1/2 teaspoon salt

1/4 teaspoon crushed hot red pepper

FOR VEGETABLES:

9 medium red potatoes, scrubbed and cut in quarters

3 large carrots, cut into 1/2-inch-long rounds

1 tablespoon extra virgin olive oil

4 ripe plum tomatoes, cut into 1/2-inch-thick rounds

2 medium onions, sliced into 1/4-inch-thick half-moons

1 teaspoon salt

1/4 teaspoon freshly ground black pepper

1 tablespoon chopped fresh parsley

1. For the chicken, position a rack in the center of the oven, and preheat the oven to 375°F. Lightly oil a roasting pan large enough to hold the chicken in one layer.

2. Lightly pound each chicken breast with the flat side of a meat pounder until it is about 1/2 inch thick. Whisk the wine, oil, oregano, garlic, salt, and hot pepper in a 13 × 9-inch glass or ceramic baking dish. Add the chicken and cover. Refrigerate and marinate for about 1 1/4 hours (but no longer than 1 1/2 hours), turning occasionally, while roasting the potatoes and carrots.

3. Toss the potatoes and carrots with the oil in a large bowl. Place them

in the roasting pan. Cover with aluminum foil and bake for 45 minutes. Uncover and bake for 15 minutes more.

4. Remove the roasting pan from the oven. Scatter the tomatoes and onions over the vegetables in the pan, add the salt and pepper, and toss together. Remove the chicken breasts from their marinade, and arrange them in the pan. Pour the marinade over all. Return to the oven, and bake until the chicken is opaque when pierced in the center with the tip of a knife, about 25 minutes. Sprinkle with the parsley, and serve hot.

• • •

Papà's Steak Pizzaiola

This is my dad's specialty. I think about him every time I make it (although I'm a lucky girl, and he's usually here in my house when I'm cooking it).

MAKES 4 SERVINGS

Two 12-ounce shell (strip) steaks, each about ³⁄₄ inch thick

³⁄₄ teaspoon salt

3 tablespoons extra virgin olive oil

2 medium onions, chopped

2 garlic cloves, minced

4 ripe plum tomatoes, cored, seeded, and diced

1 teaspoon dried oregano

¹⁄₄ teaspoon crushed hot red pepper (optional)

1 tablespoon chopped fresh parsley

1. Pat the steaks dry with a paper towel and season them with ¹⁄₂ teaspoon salt. Let stand at room temperature while making the tomato sauce.

2. Heat 2 tablespoons oil in a large skillet over medium heat. Add the onions and garlic and cook, stirring occasionally, until softened, about 3 minutes. Add the tomatoes, oregano, remaining ¹⁄₄ teaspoon salt, and

continues on page 189

the hot pepper, if using. Stir in ¼ cup water and bring to a simmer. Reduce the heat to medium-low and simmer, stirring occasionally, about 20 minutes, until the sauce thickens. During the last 5 minutes, stir in the parsley. Transfer the sauce to a bowl, and clean the skillet.

3. Heat the remaining 1 tablespoon of oil in the skillet over medium-high heat. Add the steaks to the skillet and cook about 3 minutes on each side for medium-rare. Transfer to a carving board and let stand for 5 minutes.

4. Pour out the fat in the skillet. Return the tomato sauce to the skillet and bring to a simmer, scraping up the browned bits in the skillet. Remove from the heat.

5. Hold the knife at a slight diagonal and cut the steak across the grain into ½-inch-thick slices. Arrange the steak slices on a platter. Pour the tomato sauce over the steak and serve hot.

• • •

Voluptuous Veal Piccata

MAKES 4 SERVINGS

1 pound veal scaloppine, cut into 8 pieces

¼ teaspoon salt

¼ teaspoon freshly ground black pepper

½ cup all-purpose flour

2 tablespoons extra virgin olive oil, plus more if needed

1 cup dry white wine

2 tablespoons unsalted butter

2 tablespoons fresh lemon juice

2 tablespoons drained capers

1 garlic clove, minced

1 tablespoon chopped fresh parsley

continues on page 191

1. Pound the veal cutlets with the flat side of a meat pounder until they are about 1/4 inch thick. Season with the salt and pepper. Spread the flour on a large plate. Coat both sides of the veal cutlets in the flour. Shake to remove excess flour.

2. Heat the oil in a large skillet over medium-high heat. In batches, without crowding, add the veal to the pan, and cook 1 minute on each side, until golden brown. Add more oil only if really necessary. Remove the veal from the pan and set aside.

3. Add the wine to the skillet and bring to a boil, scraping any brown bits from the bottom of the pan with a wooden spoon. Boil until reduced by half, about 2 minutes. Add the butter, lemon juice, capers, garlic, and parsley. Return the veal to the pan and cook, turning the veal in the skillet to coat with the sauce, until the veal is tender, about 1 minute more. Serve hot.

• • •

STUFFED FLOUNDER FLORENTINE

MAKES 4 SERVINGS

1 1/2 tablespoons extra virgin olive oil

1 small onion, finely chopped

1 pound baby spinach leaves, rinsed and shaken
   to remove excess water

3 tablespoons freshly grated Parmigiano-Reggiano

3 tablespoons dried Italian-seasoned bread crumbs

1/2 teaspoon salt

1/4 teaspoon freshly ground black pepper

Four 6- to 7-ounce flounder fillets

1/4 cup dry white wine

1 lemon, cut into wedges, for serving

1 tablespoon chopped fresh parsley

continues on page 192

1. Position a rack in the upper third of the oven and preheat the oven to 400°F. Lightly oil an 11 × 8-inch baking dish.

2. Heat 1 tablespoon of oil in a large saucepan over medium heat. Add the onion and cook until tender, about 5 minutes. In batches, letting the first addition wilt before adding another, add the spinach. Cook, stirring often, until the spinach begins to wilt, about 5 minutes. Drain in a colander. Using a rubber spatula, press the spinach well to remove excess liquid. Transfer to a bowl, and stir in 2 tablespoons Parmigiano, 1 tablespoon bread crumbs, $1/4$ teaspoon salt, and $1/8$ teaspoon pepper. Let stand until cool enough to handle.

3. Season the flounder fillets with the remaining $1/4$ teaspoon salt and $1/8$ teaspoon pepper. For each serving, place a fillet on the work surface, with the shinier skinned side up. Place one quarter of the spinach in the center of the fillet, shaping it into a compact log about 2 $1/2$ inches long. Fold over the right and left sides of the fillet to enclose the spinach. Arrange the flounder fillets, folded side down, in the baking dish. Drizzle the wine over the fish. Mix the remaining 2 tablespoons bread crumbs and 1 tablespoon Parmigiano. Sprinkle the bread crumb mixture over the fillets, and drizzle with the remaining $1/2$ tablespoon oil.

4. Bake until the flounder is opaque when pierced with the tip of a knife, 15 to 20 minutes. Serve hot, with the lemon wedges and a spoonful of the pan juices. Sprinkle the parsley over all.

Dreamy Desserts

We Italians love cannoli and apple cake and
panettone, but we save those sweets for special
occasions. We do still enjoy dessert, though,
and it's usually something light or fruity, or
something you can dunk in your coffee.

MAMMA ANTONIA'S
AMAZING ALMOND COOKIES

Every Italian mamma has her own special way of making almond cookies. This is my sweet mamma's. They're the best!

MAKES ABOUT 4 DOZEN

2 cups sliced blanched almonds

1 1/2 cups sugar

4 large egg whites, at room temperature

1/4 teaspoon salt

1 teaspoon vanilla extract

6 ounces semisweet, milk, or white chocolate, finely chopped

1. Position a rack in the center of the oven and preheat the oven to 350°F. Spread the almonds on a baking sheet. Bake, stirring the almonds occasionally, until lightly toasted, about 10 minutes. Cool completely.

2. Reduce the oven temperature to 325°F. Line 2 baking sheets with parchment paper.

3. Process the almonds and sugar in a food processor until finely ground. Whip the egg whites and salt in a large bowl with an electric mixer on high speed until stiff peaks form. Add the almond mixture and vanilla. Fold with a rubber spatula until combined.

4. Using a heaping teaspoon for each cookie, drop the batter onto the baking sheets, spacing them at least 2 inches apart. The cookies will spread during baking. Bake, switching the positions of the sheets from top to bottom and front to back halfway through baking, until the cookies are golden brown, about 20 minutes. Let cool on the baking sheets for 5 minutes, then transfer to a wire cooling rack to cool completely. When baking subsequent batches of cookies, be sure to use cool baking sheets.

5. Melt the chocolate in the top part of a double boiler over hot, not simmering, water. Remove from the heat and cool slightly.

continues on page 196

6. Arrange the cookies side by side on clean parchment or waxed paper. Drizzle the melted chocolate over the cookies in a pretty pattern. Cool to set the chocolate.

• • •

LEMONITA GRANITA

MAKES 4 SERVINGS

If you've ever had true Italian gelato, you know it's ice cream from angels. In Italy, though, we also perfected the healthier combination of fruit and ice. The granita was invented in Sicily and it's like a cross between a sorbet and an Italian ice. The most common flavors are lemon, mandarin orange, strawberry, coffee, almond, and mint. But my absolute favorite is lemon.

1 ¼ cups sugar

1 cup fresh lemon juice

Grated zest of 1 large lemon

Sprigs of fresh mint, for garnish

1. Bring 2 cups water and the sugar to a boil in a small saucepan, stirring just until the sugar dissolves. Let boil for 5 minutes. Add the lemon juice and zest, return to a boil, and boil for 3 minutes. Remove from the heat and cool completely.

2. Place a metal baking pan (an 8-inch square pan is perfect) in the freezer to chill. Pour the syrup into the pan. Freeze until the mixture has frozen edges, about 2 hours. Scrape the frozen edges into the mixture, and freeze again until the mixture has frozen into a slushy ice, about 2 hours longer.

3. Using the fork, scrape the granita into chilled bowls. Garnish each with a sprig of mint, and serve immediately.

After-Dinner Delights

No Italian meal would be complete without a nice hot cup of coffee at the end. Even though the Italians didn't invent coffee, they did invent *espresso* and they opened the first coffee bars in Venice in the 1700s. Espresso is a very rich coffee made by forcing water past the coffee beans at great pressure. For perfect espresso, Italian coffee beans are roasted differently than American or French. French coffee is really dark and oily. American coffee is pretty watered down. And Italian coffee is rich brown and has very little oil.

You can drink your coffee any way you like, but be warned that if you're in Italy, and you add any kind of milk or cream to your coffee after noon, you will be laughed at (milk is only for breakfast over there).

Biscotti, which means "twice cooked" in Italian, aren't the same as the thick, gooey, chewy, caramel- and candy bar–filled cookies we love so much in America. Biscotti dough is baked once, cut into long strips, and baked again, so it's crispy and almost dry. Since Italian biscotti don't have oil or butter in them like many American versions, they are much healthier and, be warned, much harder. The magic comes when you dunk your biscotti into your coffee and it comes back to life, all soft and chewy and full of flavor. Again, we keep our portions small in Italy, so we don't eat ten biscotti, but a single slice with a nice cup of coffee . . . heaven!

My girls love to help me make biscotti. Here are our favorite recipes.

BEAUTIFUL BISCOTTI

MAKES ABOUT
2 ½ DOZEN COOKIES

3 large eggs, at room temperature

1 cup granulated sugar

1 teaspoon vanilla extract

¼ teaspoon almond extract

2 ¾ cups all-purpose flour

¾ teaspoon baking powder

⅛ teaspoon salt

½ cup (2 ounces) sliced natural almonds

¼ cup confectioners' sugar, for kneading

1. Position a rack in the center of the oven and preheat the oven to 350°F. Line a large baking sheet with parchment paper.

continues on page 200

*I just love giving
you little Italian
lessons for your
everyday life. So
here's another one:
barista, the word
we use for the girl
who makes your
coffee at Starbucks,
actually means
"bartender" in
Italian.*

*And as you
leave a coffeehouse
in Italy, you
should always
say ciao ("good-
bye," pronounced
"chow") and
grazie ("thanks,"
pronounced
"GRAH-tsee-eh")
to every employee.*

2. Whip the eggs, granulated sugar, vanilla, and almond extract in a large bowl with an electric mixer on high speed until thick and pale yellow, about 3 minutes. In another bowl, stir the flour, baking powder, and salt together. Stir into the egg mixture to make a stiff, sticky dough. Stir in the almonds.

3. Sprinkle the confectioners' sugar over the work surface. Transfer the dough to the work surface, and knead gently until the dough is cohesive and loses its stickiness. Shape into a thick 8-inch log and transfer to the baking sheet. Shape the dough on the sheet into a log about 12 inches long and 2 inches wide.

4. Bake until the dough is lightly browned and cracked, and feels set when pressed on the top, about 30 minutes. Let cool on the baking sheet for 30 minutes.

5. Reduce the oven temperature to 325°F. Carefully transfer the log to a chopping board. Using a serrated knife, cut the log on a diagonal into 1/2-inch-thick slices. Arrange the slices, flat sides down, on the baking sheet. (You may need 2 baking sheets. If so, place a second oven rack in the top third of the oven.) Bake until the surfaces begin to brown, about 10 minutes. Flip the biscotti over, and bake for another 10 minutes. The biscotti will become crisper when cooled. Transfer to a wire cooling rack and cool completely.

FOR CINNAMON HAZELNUT BISCOTTI:

Substitute 3/4 cup toasted, peeled, and coarsely chopped hazelnuts for the almonds. Omit the almond extract and add 1 teaspoon ground cinnamon to the dough.

FOR ALMOND-ORANGE BISCOTTI:

Add the grated zest of 1 orange and 2 tablespoons fresh orange juice to the dough.

FOR DOUBLE CHOCOLATE BISCOTTI:

Reduce the flour to 2 1/2 cups. Add 1/4 cup unsweetened cocoa powder to the flour mixture. Stir 1 cup (6 ounces) semisweet chocolate chips into the dough.

11 ∽ Italian Dressing and Delicious Shoes

I have loved fashion since I was a little girl. I didn't always have the best clothes—we didn't have a lot of money when I was growing up because my parents left everything behind in Italy to start over in America—but I loved dressing up in anything I could find.

I got my very first Italian designer handbag from my dad when I was thirteen years old. He went to Europe to visit his family (the Italian brands are much cheaper over there!) and I asked him to bring me a Gucci purse because I just loved all the Gs (my maiden name and my married name both start with G, so I pretended the Gs were just for me). My dad doesn't know anything about purses, so I was really touched that he brought me back a tiny ivory Gucci purse with a flap close and tan Gs all over it. (I actually still have it, can you believe that? I'm saving it to give to Gia.)

I wanted to make fashion more than a hobby, so I went to school and got a degree. One of my first jobs was working as an associate buyer for Macy's in New York City. I still lived in Jersey with my parents, so I had to take two trains and three subways to work every day, but I loved it (well, I wouldn't say I "loved" the subway part—it was pretty gross, especially before Giuliani

Most people don't know this, but I actually named my third daughter Milania after the city of Milan (not after Donald Trump's newest wife, Melania, although I hear she's lovely).

The last time Joe and I took the girls to Italy, I was five months pregnant with Milania.

When we were in Milan, I decided that I just had to name her after the city, and I added an "-ia" on the end because I love all girls' names that end with an "a" (like Teresa, of course!). That child was born with fashion in her blood! Maybe she'll hit the catwalks someday like Gia rocked it at New York Fashion Week.

was the mayor). I loved being able to work in the city. Loved working with fashion. Loved making my own money so I could buy beautiful things!

I'm no one's mistress, so I'm probably not going to "die in Dior" like Kim Zolciak, but I've been blessed enough to buy pieces by my favorite designers: Dolce & Gabbana, Versace, Moschino, Roberto Cavalli, La Perla, and Miu Miu (created by Miuccia Prada, the daughter of Prada's founder). I also love the new Italian designer Cristiano Burani, and my Bravo boyfriend, Christian Siriano.

Of course, there are hundreds of wonderful designers in countries all over the world, but Italy is near the top because it treats fashion like art, the products are really well made with high-quality materials, and because they make the wearer feel a little spoiled, a little more sophisticated, and a whole lot sexier.

History of Italian Fashion

Italy has always been a major fashion force in the world, but for hundreds of years, the fanciest clothes could only be worn by (or afforded by) the rich and the royal. After World War Two, European fashion lost some of its glamour because the entire world had changed. The newly democratic governments filtered down to the way people could dress. For the first time, people dressed however they wanted, not just within their social class.

In 1951, Count Giovanni Battista Giorgini, a buyer for major American department stores, decided it was time to bring the fairy tale of fashion back, and bring it to everyone. He hosted a huge fashion show at his palace in Florence and invited an international audience. He debuted modern Italian clothes, and nobility modeled them. The idea was that every woman could dress like a princess, and still look like a modern goddess.

Even today, Italian women have a reputation for dressing really well, but I promise, it's not something you have to be born with. I can teach you style, honey. *Andiamo*! Let's go!

My dad still keeps this high school photo in his wallet. Proof that big hair is beautiful, and that I made the name necklace cool way before Carrie Bradshaw.

Teresa's Fabulicious Fashion Tips

No one, no matter who they are or what they tell you, is born with fabulous style. Everyone makes the same hideous mistakes in high school. Everyone has an awkward stage. Everyone learns by looking around them, studying, imitating, experimenting, and finding their own groove. Here are some easy ways to add glamour to your life.

Tip 1 • Don't Read Fashion Magazines

I know it seems crazy, since that's where most stylists will tell you to start, but if you're not six feet tall with an eighteen-inch waist and more money than Midas, you are only setting yourself up for frustration and disappointment. How does looking at fantasy shots of models in avant-garde clothes they don't even sell within six hundred miles of your zip code possibly help you to be more stylish?

I'm a magazine junkie, and, just like you, I can't live without my *People*, *Us*, and *In Touch*. But I've never bought a fashion magazine in my life. Never.

My Own Language

I'm sure you've figured it out by now, but my favorite word, *fabulicious*, came about because I say "fabulous" and "delicious" all the time, and somehow I just mushed them together one day and it stuck. I've taken a lot of heat for making up words (like *cleansiness*), but most people who are raised in dual-language households do that. My friend sent her daughter Hunter to speech therapy because her preschool teachers couldn't understand her, only to find out that it wasn't a speech problem but a made-up-word problem. Hunter's daddy is from Scotland and she was blending words from both cultures like "backyarden" and "umbrollie."

I think in both Italian and English, and sometimes I just go back and forth when I'm speaking without realizing it. Another of my favorite words is *skieve*—I use it like a verb to mean when something grosses me out. In Italian, *che schifo* (pronounced kay-SKEE-foe) means "how gross," so I probably picked it up from that.

I've heard that Bethenny wrote some not-so-nice things about the way I speak, but I think knowing two languages and using them interchangeably every single day is a sign of intelligence, creativity, and a super-sharp mind. Making fun of people from other cultures, maybe that is a sign of the opposite.

Don't start. It won't help you. (I'd also recommend staying away from the blogs if you happen to appear on a reality TV show. Not so good for the self-esteem . . .) Instead, walk around your city and your local mall. Visit the local boutiques. You'll see what people are wearing, what's hot this year, and what looks you like. People-watch your way into fashion do's (and don'ts).

Tip 2 • Model, Model

I don't know when I first taught my girls to say "model, model," but we probably say it ten times a day. It's just a fun little phrase that instantly makes my girls start striking fabulous poses. It's like a little reminder to bring glamour and confidence into your day no matter what you're doing.

The smiles my little girls have on when they wear something they think makes them look beautiful really do make them look beautiful, even if they're just goofing around with a kitchen towel over their hair. The same is true for big girls: you will look fabulous if you feel fabulous and believe in yourself.

One thing that Italian women share is a desire to look good all the time, even at the grocery store, even when they're gardening. Of course, you don't need to wear fancy clothes to run errands, but you should make a conscious effort to look pulled together. I don't care if you're going to the hardware store, you don't have to wear stained sweat pants or your husband's old T-shirt. Ever. (Afraid of getting your top dirty while you lug pots of flowers? There are tons of adorable boys waiting to carry your purchases all the way to your car . . . especially if you're dressed cute.)

One of the finalists on Cycle Thirteen of *America's Next Top Model*, Laura Kirkpatrick from Kentucky, is so cute, and I just love her attitude. She's from a really small town, but she's been modeling her butt off ever since she could walk. She says she sashayed down the aisles of her local Wal-Mart just like it was a runway.

Remind yourself to "model, model" every day, even if it just inspires you to add a fancy headband or wear pretty earrings with the outfit you already had on.

Tip 3 • Tailor Made

Celebrities and models look extra great when they go out because they get couture clothes: clothes sewn just for them. The rest of us are stuck picking it off the rack and hoping it fits our unique shape. A hundred and fifty years ago, everyone made their own clothes, so each piece was fitted just for your body (usually by your mamma). Once clothes started to be mass-produced, they made up sizes they thought would fit most women and just left it up to the consumer. Unfortunately for most of us that means walking away from a piece of clothing we love because it's just too long/big/doesn't hang right/or won't button over the twins.

There are more than a hundred million women in America and we're

certainly not all the same size. But I think we've been tricked into thinking we have to fit perfectly into what's on the shelves, or go home depressed.

This stops right now! Consider the clothes you see in the stores as samples, just like the patterns they make on *Project Runway*. You've seen how much the dress changes once their model comes in. Get the pieces you love and then take them to a tailor.

Almost every dry cleaner has a tailor on staff or can refer you to one. It's not as expensive as you think. It's not like getting an outfit custom-made for you from scratch. Tailoring can cost as little as twenty dollars (and it's free in many department stores!), and it can make all the difference in how your clothes fit you and how you feel in them.

I also have friends that can't quite sew but they can sure "Project Runway" an outfit to fit them for a party. You've seen what they do: duct tape, hot glue guns, pins . . . Who's going to see the inside of your hem? During photo shoots, even the models are covered with clips and safety pins from the back to make every fold and every crease look just perfect from the front. You deserve the same!

$\mathit{Tip}\ 4$ • Simply Remember Your Favorite Thing

This is the most important piece of advice I can give you: when you're look-ing for a fabulous outfit, find one thing you love-love-love and build every-thing around it. Most people think they have to find the dress or the skirt and then throw accessories and shoes on to match as an afterthought. Instead, approach dressing the same way an interior designer approaches a new room. Dina (who is a genius decorator) will find one piece in a room that the owner really loves, whether it's a painting or a chandelier or just a little knickknack, and she'll build the whole room around it.

Do the same thing. When a hot necklace, or amazing shoes, or a great shirt catches your eye, buy it, and then build your entire look around it. You'll find successful outfits much faster, and you'll feel better wearing them because you are focusing on the original thing you loved the most.

$\mathit{Tip}\ 5$ • Walk Like an Italian

I mean this in two ways: walk with confidence, and walk as much as you can.

Walk like an Italian!

In Italy, women walk everywhere (and in high heels). When I first got my Peg Perego stroller for Gabriella, I realized the damn thing didn't have a cup holder. Some fancy Italian stroller! Then I realized why: in Italy they don't have cup holders in anything: not strollers and not even cars. It's because Italians don't eat on the run. They don't grab a huge whipped-creamed coffee drink and then rush to their next location. Italians sit, eat, and enjoy. And in between, they walk. A lot.

Walk as much as you possibly can. Park farther away from the store's entrance (it will save your car from nasty dings anyway). Park down the street from your hair salon. Walk all the way to the park, library, or store. Every little step will help you look ass-tastic!

Also, walk confidently. Models are beautiful, even though they all look so different (and sometimes quite alien-like). They're beautiful because they walk like they are. You do the same, no matter where you are or what you're doing. Sway those hips, and shake that ass, because Baby Doll, you are beautiful, too!

How to Fake It on Any Budget

Of course, not everyone can afford the top Italian designers—and unless you're the pope, you can't afford them all the time—but there are tons of ways to dress in beautiful clothes without breaking your bank. I'm not a big fan of faking anything, so I am not suggesting you go buy knockoffs or cheap imitations. They won't look good and I promise they won't last long, so they're a waste of your money.

Instead, try to invest in just a few amazing pieces that you can add to regular, nondesigner clothes to bring everything up a notch. Look for classic pieces, like black pants or a nice blouse, and make sure they're made of natural materials.

I also think accessories make the outfit, and every girl deserves a beautiful handbag, a great pair of shoes, and some gorgeous jewelry.

Now, the jewelry doesn't have to be dripping with diamonds to be hot (not all of us are as lucky as Jill Zarin to have a giant "baby" diamond on her

Italian Horns

One of my favorite accessories is the Italian horn necklace (called *corno* or *cornicello* for "little horn" in Italian). You might have seen me buy one at a boutique near my house on Season One. I love them not just because they're big and colorful and make a statement, but because Italians believe they help keep away the evil eye.

The evil eye is the idea that a person can harm you or your family by looking too long and too longingly at you or at them. It might seem like superstition to some, but many, many people believe in it, including modern Christians, Jews, and Muslims. There is a word for the evil eye in Hebrew, Yiddish, Italian, Spanish, Arabic, and Farsi. It's even mentioned in the Old Testament.

Me, I love necklaces that remind me of my Italian heritage, I like how pretty they are, and I could use all the help against evil I can get. Who couldn't?

finger and an even bigger "mamma" diamond in the safe). But you can find amazing necklaces and bracelets and earrings at local boutiques or department stores that will dress up even a pair of jeans. Forget thin gold chains or tiny diamonds. Those don't make a statement anyway. You want sparkle and statement, patterns and big, fun pieces.

Where can you find real designer shoes and handbags for a discount? Look on the Internet, especially sites that recycle barely worn clothing. Discount retailers like Loehmann's have great designer specials. And every department store on earth has a yearly sale. There's also the outlet malls. There are Salvatore Ferragamo designer outlet shoe stores all over the country. Same with Gucci, Armani, Dolce & Gabbana, Versace, Prada, and Diesel (Italian designer jeans that make your ass look amazing).

Best Italian Recipes for Little Black Dress Emergencies

Even if you're eating right and exercising, and you have a few great pieces of clothing in your closet that you know look slamming on you, everyone has a fashion emergency. Maybe you injured yourself and couldn't get around like normal (except from the couch to the pantry). Maybe it's your time of the month. Maybe you just got back from a glorious, all-bets-are-off vacation. Whatever the case, every girl has faced the special occasion when she has to fit into her little black dress (or skinny jeans) in a big fat hurry.

As you know, I'm never an advocate of starving yourself, using crazy diet aids, or eating weird stuff. But thankfully, there are Italian meals that are still amazing and super-filling, but healthier than most. We won't call these "diet" foods, but these are my favorite recipes for when I have an LBD emergency.

FENNEL SALAD

MAKES 4 SERVINGS

1 large fennel bulb

1 tablespoon fresh lemon juice

1 tablespoon red wine vinegar

$1/4$ teaspoon salt

$1/8$ teaspoon freshly ground black pepper

2 tablespoons extra virgin olive oil

1 tablespoon chopped fresh parsley

1. Cut the fennel in half lengthwise. Cut out the tough triangular core at the bottom of the bulb. Cut the fennel crosswise into very thin slices. (You can use a mandoline or plastic V-slicer if you wish.) You should have about 4 cups sliced fennel.

2. Whisk the lemon juice, vinegar, salt, and pepper in a large bowl. Gradually whisk in the oil. Add the fennel and toss well. Sprinkle with the parsley.

3. Serve immediately, or refrigerate for an hour or so and serve chilled.

• • •

PANZANELLA SALAD

MAKES 8 SERVINGS

CROUTONS

$1/3$ cup extra virgin olive oil

2 garlic cloves, minced

$1/8$ teaspoon salt

1 loaf day-old crusty Italian or French bread,
   cut into 1-inch cubes

SALAD

¼ **cup balsamic vinegar**

¼ **teaspoon salt**

¼ **teaspoon freshly ground black pepper**

¼ **cup extra virgin olive oil**

4 large ripe tomatoes, cored, seeded, and cut into ½-inch dice

4 ounces fresh mozzarella, cut into bite-sized cubes

½ **cup pitted and chopped kalamata olives**

½ **red onion, finely chopped**

10 fresh basil leaves, torn into pieces

1 tablespoon drained capers

1. To make the croutons, position a rack in the center of the oven and pre-heat the oven to 400°F.

2. Whisk the oil, garlic, and salt together in a large bowl. Add the bread cubes and toss well. Spread on a rimmed baking sheet. Bake, stirring occa-sionally, until golden brown, about 10 minutes. Let cool.

3. To make the salad, whisk the vinegar, salt, and pepper in a small bowl. Gradually whisk in the oil. Combine the croutons, tomatoes, mozzarella, olives, onion, basil, and capers in a large bowl. Add the dressing and toss well. Let stand for 20 minutes before serving.

GIARDINO MINESTRONE

MAKES ABOUT
3 QUARTS, 12 SERVINGS

2 tablespoons extra virgin olive oil

1 medium onion, diced

1 medium carrot, cut into 1/2-inch dice

2 garlic cloves, minced

5 cups canned low-sodium vegetable or chicken broth

4 ripe plum tomatoes, cored, seeded, and diced

1/2 teaspoon dried oregano

1/4 teaspoon salt

1/4 teaspoon freshly ground black pepper

One 19-ounce can cannellini (white kidney) beans,
    drained and rinsed

4 ounces green beans, trimmed and cut into 1/2-inch pieces

2 medium zucchini, cut into 1/2-inch dice

1 cup uncooked small shell pasta (conchiglie)

1 tablespoon chopped fresh basil

1 tablespoon chopped fresh parsley

1/2 cup freshly grated Parmigiano-Reggiano

1. Heat the oil in a soup pot over medium heat. Add the onion and carrot, and cook until they begin to soften, about 5 minutes. Add the garlic and cook until fragrant, about 1 minute. Stir in the broth, 2 cups water, the tomatoes, oregano, salt, and pepper. Bring to a boil over high heat. Reduce the heat to medium-low and simmer for 45 minutes.

2. Add the cannellini beans, green beans, zucchini, and pasta, and return to a simmer over high heat. Return the heat to medium-low, and simmer until the pasta is tender, about 10 minutes. During the last few minutes, add the basil and parsley. Sprinkle in the cheese, and serve hot.

Pasta Umbria

MAKES 6 SERVINGS

4 tablespoons extra virgin olive oil

1 small red onion, diced

2 garlic cloves, minced

1 medium zucchini, cut into $1/2$-inch cubes

1 medium eggplant, cut into 1-inch cubes

1 red bell pepper, cored, seeded, and cut into $1/2$-inch dice

$1/4$ teaspoon salt

$1/4$ teaspoon crushed hot red pepper

1 pound orecchiette or conchiglie (large shell) pasta

3 tablespoons Audriana's Pesto (page 131)

$1/2$ cup (2 ounces) shredded ricotta salata cheese

1. Heat 2 tablespoons of oil in a large saucepan over medium heat. Add the onion and garlic and cook, stirring occasionally, until the onion softens, about 3 minutes. Add the remaining oil, and heat. Add the zucchini, eggplant, bell pepper, salt, and hot pepper. Cook, stirring often, until the vegetables have cooked into a thick, tender mixture, about 20 minutes.

2. Meanwhile, bring a large pot of lightly salted water to a boil over high heat. Add the pasta and cook according to the package directions until almost al dente. (The pasta will cook further in the sauce.)

3. Drain the pasta, reserving $3/4$ cup of the pasta cooking water. Transfer the pasta to the sauce. Add the pesto. Stir in enough of the pasta water to make a light sauce that clings to the pasta. Reduce the heat to low and cook until the pasta is just al dente, about 3 minutes. Remove from the heat. Sprinkle with the cheese, and serve hot.

SKINNY SNAPPER

MAKES 4 SERVINGS

1 tablespoon plus 2 teaspoons extra virgin olive oil

1 medium onion, sliced into thin half-moons

1 small green bell pepper, cored, seeded,
   and cut into $\frac{1}{2}$-inch-wide strips

2 garlic cloves, finely chopped

$\frac{3}{4}$ teaspoon salt

$\frac{1}{2}$ teaspoon freshly ground black pepper

2 large tomatoes, cut in eighths

Four 5- to 6-ounce red snapper fillets

4 thin lemon slices

1 tablespoon chopped fresh parsley

1. Position a rack in the center of the oven and preheat the oven to 400°F.

2. Heat 1 tablespoon of oil in a large ovenproof skillet over medium heat.
Add the onion, bell pepper, and garlic, and season with $\frac{1}{2}$ teaspoon salt and
$\frac{1}{4}$ teaspoon pepper. Cook, stirring often, until softened, about 5 minutes.
Add the tomatoes and mix well.

3. Season the fillets with the remaining $\frac{1}{4}$ teaspoon salt and $\frac{1}{4}$ teaspoon
pepper. Place the fillets, skin side down, on the vegetables in the skillet.
Place a lemon slice on each fillet. Drizzle with the remaining 2 teaspoons oil.
Place the skillet in the oven and bake until the fish is opaque when pierced
with the tip of a knife, about 10 minutes. Sprinkle with the parsley, and
serve hot.

12 Love-Love-Love

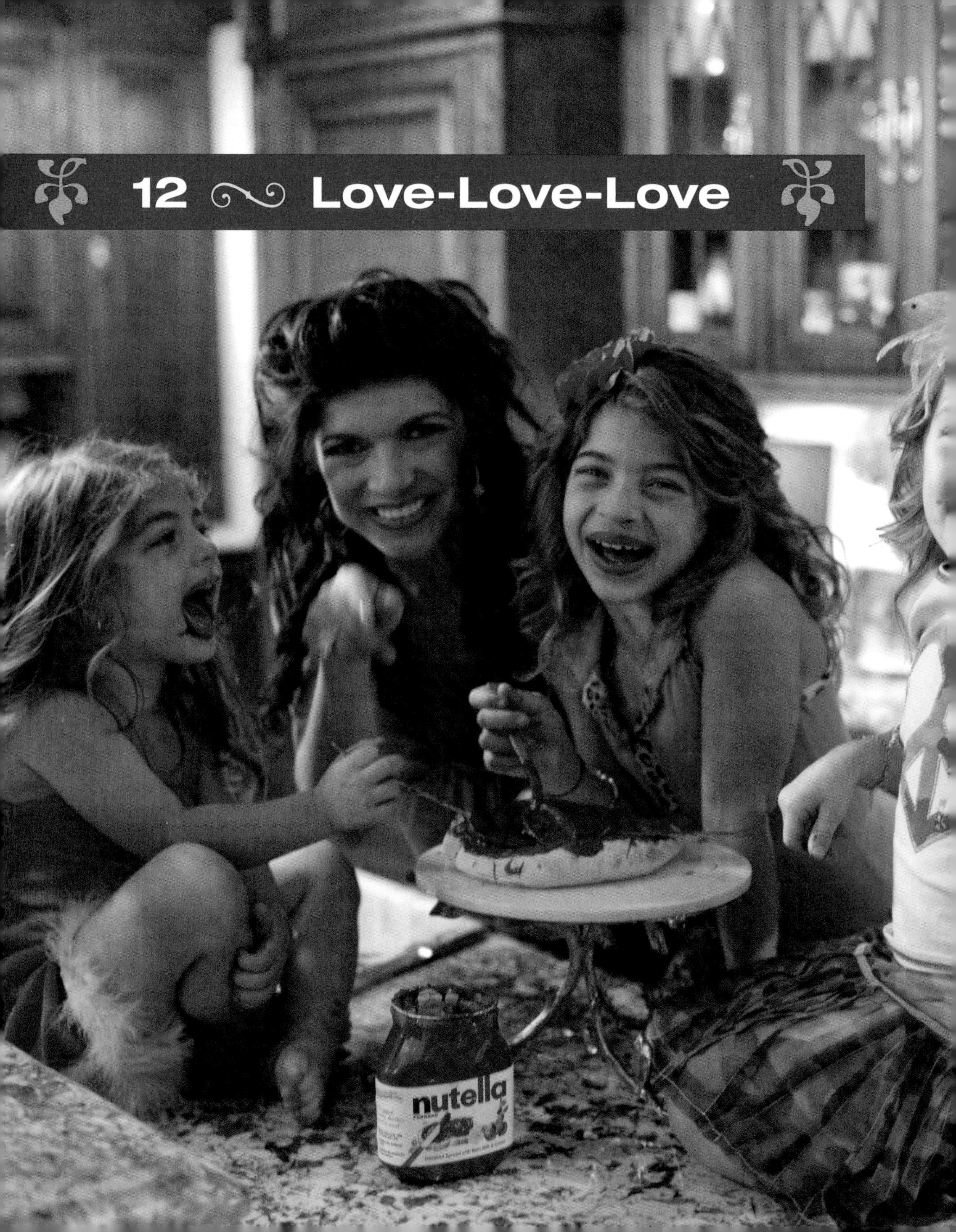

I certainly do not have a perfect life. Being married for ten years and having four little girls is not easy. Sometimes I yell. Sometimes Joe and I argue. But for the most part, I'm a really happy person. No matter what's going on, I just try to appreciate every day.

I've always thought that happy people lived longer and healthier lives. I've seen reports that people in a relationship are happier and healthier than those who are alone, and happy people are more immune to even the common cold. It just makes sense. But it wasn't until I found Dr. David Snowdon's research on the brains of Catholic nuns that I found my evidence.

For fifteen years, he studied 678 School Sisters of Notre Dame from the ages of 75 to 106. Here's the creepy part: each nun who participated in the study agreed to donate her brain to science when she died. As that happened, and they studied the brains (and compiled all their research of the nuns while they were alive), they found that the happiest nuns had the healthiest brains. Dr. Snowdon's "Nun Study" concluded that, "those who are hopeful, happy, and optimistic in attitude live much longer." I knew it!

Count Blessings, Not Calories

Just like I've never seen a runner or a woman in labor with a smile on their face, I've never met a happy dieter. When you deprive yourself of wonderful food, you're miserable, and the misery hormones slow down your metabolism so you don't lose weight, and then you're twice as miserable.

We've looked at some of the reasons Italians live longer, healthier lives: because of the fresh, healthy food they eat, and how they eat it, and because celebrating is part of our culture.

No one can control what family they're dropped into, what size body they're genetically gifted with, or what fortunes or misfortunes might come their way. But if we all took as much time counting our blessings as we do counting calories, we'd all be a lot healthier. Maybe that's a good idea: every time you are tempted to look at the nutrition facts of a food, remind yourself of the ounces of blessings and grams of happiness you've had, do have, will have, and deserve to have.

Let me help you begin counting your blessings: you're now officially one of my hot Italian friends, you care enough about your health and your family that you bought this book to learn a new way of cooking and eating, and I adore you!

Sexy Is as Sexy Does

One of the reasons I love the title of my book is because it makes me feel happy and sexy just to say it out loud. I don't like to use the word *skinny* to refer to a person, or the way a person should be. I think really skinny can actually be kind of gross. I love curves. Since I had Audriana, my ass is bigger, and I love it (isn't it so great that we live in an age where juicy asses are a good thing?). But "skinny jeans" is a happy place. The size of my mom's skinny jeans isn't the same as mine, but those are the pants that make us happy. We're not supposed to all look the same. But we can all be healthy, fabulous, and sexy-sexy-sexy! You are sexy. The way you flip your hair is sexy. The way you smile is sexy. The way you move is sexy. Sexy is all about attitude, not size, and sister, we've got some to spare!

Recipes for Romance

For those days when we're not feeling particularly sexy (and it happens to all of us!), I've created some special romantic recipes to relight your fire. Pour yourself a glass of wine, remember that you're my friend and that makes you fabulous, and cook yourself sexy!

SPAGHETTI ALL'UBRIACO (DRUNKEN SPAGHETTI)

MAKES 6 SERVINGS

I love-love-love this recipe because you know it tastes great from the title. Drunken Spaghetti. What's more fun that that?

Now, most people make their drunken spaghetti with red wine. The wine soaks into the noodles and makes them dark red and runny, and, in my opinion, as good as it might taste, it is not good looking. Of course, I'm all about adding wine to my pasta, so I created a variation that uses white wine and Milania's Marinara Sauce. Salute!

Milania's Marinara Sauce (see page 119)

One 750-ml bottle Chardonnay

1 pound spaghetti

½ cup (2 ounces) freshly grated Parmigiano-Reggiano, for serving

1. Bring the marinara and 1 cup of wine to a simmer in a medium saucepan over medium heat. Reduce the heat to low, and simmer until slightly thickened, about 20 minutes. Keep warm.

2. Meanwhile, pour the remaining wine into a large pot, add 3½ quarts lightly salted water, and bring to a boil. Add the spaghetti and cook according to the package directions until al dente.

3. Drain the spaghetti and return to the pot. Add the sauce and mix well. Serve hot, with the cheese passed on the side.

SICILIAN STEAK

Here's why my Sicilian steak makes me feel super sexy: when I think of Sicily, I automatically think about the cliffside city of Taormina. You cannot imagine how spectacular it is: it's all hilly and green, Mount Etna is steaming in the distance, the sapphire-blue ocean is everywhere, and the best resorts allow you to pretty much walk on the water. (There's an amazing film festival in Taormina every year where they show movies in a 2,300-year-old open-air Greek-Roman amphitheater. It's where Transformers *had its world premiere.) The most beautiful resort in Taormina is the Grand Hotel Atlantis Bay, which makes me think of the equally beautiful Atlantis Resort in the Bahamas. Joe and I got engaged there (we couldn't afford to fly all the way to Italy to get engaged), so you can see how Atlantis + Sicily + Steak = Sexy in my book. Try it out and see what magic you can conjure up yourself!*

2 (1 pound each) shell steaks, cut about 1 inch thick

¼ cup extra virgin olive oil

2 garlic cloves, minced

⅓ cup dried bread crumbs

2 tablespoons freshly grated Parmigiano-Reggiano

1 teaspoon dried oregano

¼ teaspoon salt

¼ teaspoon freshly ground black pepper

1. Trim the excess fat from the perimeter of each steak. Combine the oil and garlic in a 13 × 9-inch glass or ceramic baking dish. Place the steaks in the baking dish, and let stand at room temperature for 30 minutes, turning the steak over after 15 minutes.

2. Mix the bread crumbs, cheese, oregano, salt, and pepper together in another shallow dish. Remove the steaks from the oil, letting the oil cling

to the steaks. Dip each steak into the bread crumb mixture, patting to coat both sides. Let stand 10 minutes to set the crumbs.

3. Position a broiler rack 6 to 8 inches from the source of heat, and preheat the broiler. (If the steaks cook too close to the heat, the crust will burn.) Lightly oil the rack. Place the steaks on the rack and broil until the crust is lightly browned, about 3 1/2 minutes. If the crust begins to scorch, move to the next lowest rung in the oven or broiler away from the heat source. Turn the steaks and cook until the other side is browned, about 3 1/2 minutes more for medium-rare meat.

4. Transfer to a platter and let stand 3 minutes. Cut across the grain into 1/2-inch-thick slices and serve.

JUICY BITS FROM *Joe*

Now Teresa telling you that we got engaged at Atlantis in the Bahamas is a big deal, because our families don't know this. We told them we drove up to the Hamptons to get engaged, but the truth is, we used to sneak down to the Bahamas every so often for a romantic getaway.

The weekend I planned to propose was actually my birthday, so we invited a bunch of our friends to go to the Bahamas with us. We were all dressed up, I was thinking about proposing to her, and she surprised *me* with a big birthday party! She had our whole room filled with balloons and happy-birthday signs. I was blown away.

That night, we went to dinner and I had this big box with her ring in my sock. It was a real pain keeping it from her. After we said goodnight to everyone, we walked along the beach holding hands, looking at the sea. I stopped by this big rock, got down on one knee, pulled the box out of my sock (it was right there when I was bending down, see?), and proposed. She cried, of course, and said yes, and the rest is history.

LUSCIOUS LINGUINE WITH MANILA CLAMS

MAKES 6 SERVINGS

This is my absolute, hands-down favorite Italian dish. It's the first one I ever really perfected and I still make it all the time. It's super easy, but something about it, steaming the clams open, is just so earthy and sensual. And of course, it's delicious!

2 1/2 pounds Manila or littleneck clams

1/3 cup extra virgin olive oil

3 garlic cloves, minced

2/3 cup dry white wine

1/8 teaspoon salt

1/8 teaspoon crushed hot red pepper

1 pound linguine

2 tablespoons unsalted butter

1 tablespoon chopped fresh parsley

1. Soak the clams in a large bowl of cold salted water for 20 minutes so they can expel any sand. Scrub the clams well under cold running water. Throw away any clams that are gaping open.

2. Heat the oil and garlic in a large saucepan over medium heat until the garlic is golden, about 3 minutes. Add the wine, salt, and hot pepper, and bring to a boil. Cook until reduced by half, about 3 minutes. Set aside.

3. Bring a large pot of lightly salted water to a boil over high heat. Add the linguine and cook according to the package instructions until al dente.

4. While the linguine is cooking, add the clams to the wine mixture in the saucepan. Cover tightly and return to high heat. Cook, occasionally shaking the pot, until the clams open, about 6 minutes. Remove from the heat. Discard any unopened clams. Add the butter; shake the pot until the butter melts.

5. Drain the linguine. Return the linguine to the pot. Add the clam sauce and mix gently. Sprinkle with the parsley, toss gently, and serve hot.

Simple, Sexy Desserts

I couldn't leave you without a sweet taste in your mouth, so to end our time together, I'm going to give you my favorite sexy desserts. They're really simple, not crazy in the calorie department, and I promise, you will have some fun with these.

FRESH FRUIT WITH BEAUTIFUL BALSAMIC GLAZE

MAKES 4 SERVINGS

This is a fabulous dessert that just lends itself to sexiness. Anything you can pour over fresh fruit and feed to someone, anything you can use your fingers for and lick the extra sauce off, is just begging for romance.

You can drizzle this over just about any fruit (my favorite is pineapple).

2 tablespoons balsamic vinegar

2 tablespoons light brown sugar

2 cups sliced fresh strawberries

2 large oranges, peeled and cut into segments

1. Bring the vinegar and brown sugar just to a boil in a small saucepan over medium heat, stirring to dissolve the sugar. Immediately remove from the heat, and let cool.

2. Combine the strawberries and oranges in a large bowl. Spoon into dessert bowls, drizzle with the glaze, and serve.

FRESH STRAWBERRIES AND SAMBUCA

This is an Italian classic, mixing strawberries with Sambuca. It's super easy to make, but the fun is in serving it to your special someone.

1 ½ pounds fresh strawberries, hulled

¼ cup sugar

⅓ cup Sambuca

Place the strawberries in a large bowl. Sprinkle with the sugar and toss gently. Pour in the Sambuca, and toss again. Let stand at room temperature to intoxicate the berries, about 10 minutes. Spoon into bowls and serve.

PIZZA NUTELLA

This is Joe's favorite dessert, and if you have some pizza dough on hand, it's a snap to whip up. Nutella is just the yummiest, creamiest, sexiest spread ever!

Bread flour, for rolling the dough

1 ball Old World Pizza Dough (page 141)

3 tablespoons chocolate-hazelnut spread, such as Nutella

1 tablespoon confectioners' sugar

1. Position a rack in the center of the oven and preheat the oven to 375°F. Line a baking sheet with parchment paper.

continues on page 235

Yummy, delicious!

2. On a lightly floured work surface, roll the dough into a 10-inch round. Carefully fold it in half, leaving it loosely filled with air in the middle. Use a fork to seal the edges, but don't deflate the dough.

3. Bake until the pizza is golden brown, about 15 minutes. Remove from the oven and let cool until warm, at least 5 minutes. The pizza should be warm, not hot, or the Nutella will melt too much (and you might burn your mouth).

4. With a serrated knife, cut open the flat end of the dough to make a pocket. Spread the inside of the pocket with Nutella. Sift confectioners' sugar over the top of the pocket. Cut vertically into 6 pieces, and serve warm.

A Parting Shot

The *Real Housewives* girls and I got invited to the *Sex and the City* movie premiere, and it was so much fun. One of my favorite scenes was when Samantha covered herself in sushi and lay on the dining room table as a surprise for Smith. That just struck me as such a fun way to bring food and romance together. I think I'm going to try it some night (when the kids are away, of course!) with some deconstructed Pizza Nutella. I leave the rest up to your imagination, but I hope I've inspired you to embrace your inner Italian goddess, taught you how to incorporate healthy cooking into your life, and given you a few reasons to smile, giggle, or gasp along the way.

Shake it up *Skinny Italian* style, Baby Doll,
because you are FABULOUS!

Nutritional Information

1 gram fiber
1 gram protein
302 milligrams sodium

SAUTÉED ZUCCHINI "SPAGHETTI" WITH PINE NUTS, PAGE 86

Each serving:
79 calories
5 grams carbohydrate
7 grams fat
1 gram saturated fat
0 milligrams cholesterol
1 gram fiber
2 grams protein
156 milligrams sodium

Chapter 6: AND GOD SAID "LET THERE BE PASTA." AND THERE WAS. AND IT WAS GOOD.

TERESA'S FAVORITE TAGLIATELLE, PAGE 106

Each serving:
423 calories
60 grams carbohydrate
13 grams fat
4 grams saturated fat
20 milligrams cholesterol
7 grams fiber
15 grams protein
324 milligrams sodium

BUCATINI ALL'AMATRICIANA, PAGE 109

Each serving:
470 calories
60 grams carbohydrate
17 grams fat
6 grams saturated fat
19 milligrams cholesterol
4 grams fiber
16 grams protein
508 milligrams sodium

FARFALLE CON PISELLI, PAGE 110

Each serving:
348 calories
62 grams carbohydrate
6 grams fat
2 grams saturated fat
9 milligrams cholesterol
4 grams fiber
12 grams protein
123 milligrams sodium

PASTA CACIO E PEPE (PASTA WITH ROMANO CHEESE AND BLACK PEPPER), PAGE 112

Each serving:
434 calories
57 grams carbohydrate
11 grams fat
7 grams saturated fat
24 milligrams cholesterol
3 grams fiber
20 grams protein
713 milligrams sodium

PENNE WITH PORTOBELLO MUSHROOM SAUCE, PAGE 113

Each serving:
380 calories
60 grams carbohydrate
8 grams fat
2 grams saturated fat
6 milligrams cholesterol
3 grams fiber
14 grams protein
205 milligrams sodium

Chapter 7: THE SECRET'S IN THE SAUCE

BASIC TOMATO SAUCE, AKA "THE QUICKIE," PAGE 117

[sauce only=6 servings]
Each serving (generous 1/2 cup):
53 calories
7 grams carbohydrate
3 grams fat
0 grams saturated fat

0 milligrams cholesterol
2 grams fiber
2 grams protein
275 milligrams sodium

[sauce with 1 pound pasta=6 servings]
Each serving:
344 calories
64 grams carbohydrate
4 grams fat
1 gram saturated fat
0 milligrams cholesterol
5 grams fiber
12 grams protein
277 milligrams sodium

MILANIA'S MARINARA SAUCE, PAGE 119

[sauce only=6 servings]
Each serving (generous 1/2 cup):
110 calories
12 grams carbohydrate
5 grams fat
1 gram saturated fat
0 milligrams cholesterol
3 grams fiber
3 grams protein
376 milligrams sodium

[sauce with 1 pound pasta=6 servings]
Each serving:
401 calories
68 grams carbohydrate
7 grams fat
1 gram saturated fat
0 milligrams cholesterol
6 grams fiber
14 grams protein
378 milligrams sodium

GABRIELLA'S BOLOGNESE SAUCE, PAGE 120

[sauce only=12 servings]
Each serving (1/2 cup):
136 calories
5 grams carbohydrate
8 grams fat
2 grams saturated fat
29 milligrams cholesterol
1 gram fiber

8 grams protein
265 milligrams sodium

[sauce with 2 pounds pasta=12 servings]
Each serving:
427 calories
62 grams carbohydrate
9 grams fat
3 grams saturated fat
29 milligrams cholesterol
5 grams fiber
18 grams protein
267 milligrams sodium

GIA'S NAPOLETANO SAUCE, PAGE 121

[sauce only=9 servings]
Each serving (generous 1/2 cup):
255 calories
7 grams carbohydrate
13 grams fat
4 grams saturated fat
66 milligrams cholesterol
2 grams fiber
24 grams protein
661 milligrams sodium

[sauce with 1 1/2 pounds pasta=
9 servings]
Each serving:
547 calories
64 grams carbohydrate
15 grams fat
4 grams saturated fat
66 milligrams cholesterol
5 grams fiber
35 grams protein
663 milligrams sodium

DANIELLE'S PUTTANESCA SAUCE, PAGE 123

[sauce only=6 servings]
Each serving (generous 1/2 cup):
120 calories
9 grams carbohydrate
9 grams fat
1 gram saturated fat
0 milligrams cholesterol
2 grams fiber

2 grams protein
508 milligrams sodium

[sauce with 1 pound pasta=6 servings]
Each serving:
411 calories
66 grams carbohydrate
11 grams fat
2 grams saturated fat
0 milligrams cholesterol
5 grams fiber
13 grams protein
510 milligrams sodium

ARRABBIATA, THE ANGRY SAUCE, PAGE 125

[sauce only=6 servings]
Each serving (generous 1/2 cup):
83 calories
9 grams carbohydrate
5 grams fat
1 gram saturated fat
0 milligrams cholesterol
2 grams fiber
2 grams protein
277 milligrams sodium

[sauce with 1 pound pasta=6 servings]
Each serving:
374 calories
66 grams carbohydrate
7 grams fat
1 gram saturated fat
0 milligrams cholesterol
6 grams fiber
13 grams protein
279 milligrams sodium

SKINNY PASTA AL BURRO, PAGE 128

Each serving:
351 calories
37 grams carbohydrate
16 grams fat
6 grams saturated fat
63 milligrams cholesterol
5 grams fiber
15.25 grams protein
464 milligrams sodium

AUDRIANA'S PESTO, PAGE 131

[sauce only=12 servings]
Each serving (generous tablespoon):
154 calories
1 gram carbohydrate
16 grams fat
3 grams saturated fat
3 milligrams cholesterol
0 grams fiber
2 grams protein
100 milligrams sodium

[sauce with 2 pounds pasta=12 servings]
Each serving:
446 calories
58 grams carbohydrate
18 grams fat
3 grams saturated fat
3 milligrams cholesterol
4 grams fiber
13 grams protein
102 milligrams sodium

Chapter 8: PIZZA! PIZZA!

OLD WORLD PIZZA DOUGH, PAGE 141

[1/4 of 1 pizza dough]
Each serving:
118 calories
17 grams carbohydrate
5 grams fat
1 gram saturated fat
0 milligrams cholesterol
1 gram fiber
3 grams protein
145 milligrams sodium

PIZZA MARGHERITA , PAGE 144

[1/4 of pizza]
Each serving:
185 calories
21 grams carbohydrate
9 grams fat
2 grams saturated fat
5 milligrams cholesterol
1 gram fiber
6 grams protein
157 milligrams sodium

PIZZA GUIDICE, PAGE 147

[¼ of pizza]
Each serving:
187 calories
21 grams carbohydrate
9 grams fat
2 grams saturated fat
4 milligrams cholesterol
1 gram fiber
6 grams protein
261 milligrams sodium

PIZZA WITH ANCHOVIES AND GARLIC, PAGE 148

[¼ of pizza]
Each serving:
203 calories
21 grams carbohydrate
12 grams fat
2 grams saturated fat
1 milligram cholesterol
1 gram fiber
4 grams protein
221 milligrams sodium

PIZZA NAPOLETANA, PAGE 151

[¼ of pizza]
Each serving:
213 calories
22 grams carbohydrate
11 grams fat
2 grams saturated fat
7 milligrams cholesterol
1 gram fiber
7 grams protein
386 milligrams sodium

PIZZA AL PROSCIUTTO, PAGE 152

[¼ of pizza]
Each serving:
251 calories
22 grams carbohydrate
14 grams fat
4 grams saturated fat
18 milligrams cholesterol
1 gram fiber
9 grams protein
487 milligrams sodium

PIZZA WITH ITALIAN SAUSAGE, PAGE 153

[¼ of pizza]
Each serving:
270 calories
24 grams carbohydrate
16 grams fat
4 grams saturated fat
22 milligrams cholesterol
2 grams fiber
8 grams protein
355 milligrams sodium

Chapter 10: THE ART OF EATING

BELLISSIMO BELLINIS, PAGE 172

Each serving:
117 calories
7 grams carbohydrate
0 grams fat
0 grams saturated fat
0 milligrams cholesterol
0 grams fiber
0 grams protein
6 milligrams sodium

LAZY BELLINIS, PAGE 174

Each serving:
177 calories
3 grams carbohydrate
0 grams fat
0 grams saturated fat
0 milligrams cholesterol
0 grams fiber
0 grams protein
7 milligrams sodium

HOMEMADE LIMONCELLO, PAGE 175

Each serving:
152 calories
17 grams carbohydrate
0 grams fat
0 grams saturated fat
0 milligrams cholesterol
0 grams fiber
0 grams protein
0 milligrams sodium

DINA'S VIRGIN MIMOSA, PAGE 176

Each serving:
28 calories
6 grams carbohydrate
0 grams fat
0 grams saturated fat
0 milligrams cholesterol
0 grams fiber
0 grams protein
1 milligram sodium

BRUSCHETTA CLASSICA, PAGE 178

Each serving:
92 calories
11 grams carbohydrate
4 grams fat
1 gram saturated fat
0 milligrams cholesterol
1 gram fiber
2 grams protein
215 milligrams sodium

BRUSCHETTA E PROSCIUTTO, PAGE 180

Each serving:
118 calories
10 grams carbohydrate
7 grams fat
2 grams saturated fat
10 milligrams cholesterol
1 gram fiber
4 grams protein
328 milligrams sodium

CAPONATA BRUSCHETTA, PAGE 181

Each serving:
92 calories
13 grams carbohydrate
3 grams fat
1 gram saturated fat
0 milligrams cholesterol
2 grams fiber
2 grams protein
285 milligrams sodium

BALSAMIC GARLIC BITES, PAGE 182

Each serving:
34 calories
4 grams carbohydrate
2 grams fat
0 grams saturated fat
0 milligrams cholesterol
0 grams fiber
1 gram protein
3 milligrams sodium

SALERNO STUFFED MUSHROOMS, PAGE 182

Each serving:
117 calories
8 grams carbohydrate
8 grams fat
2 grams saturated fat
4 milligrams cholesterol
1 gram fiber
4 grams protein
211 milligrams sodium

ONE-PAN OVEN-ROASTED CHICKEN FEAST, PAGE 186

Each serving:
510 calories
49 grams carbohydrate
16 grams fat
3 grams saturated fat
101 milligrams cholesterol
7 grams fiber
45 grams protein
693 milligrams sodium

PAPÀ'S STEAK PIZZAIOLA, PAGE 187

Each serving:
383 calories
8 grams carbohydrate
23 grams fat
7 grams saturated fat
82 milligrams cholesterol
2 grams fiber
35 grams protein
512 milligrams sodium

VOLUPTUOUS VEAL PICCATA, PAGE 189

Each serving:
334 calories
11 grams carbohydrate
16 grams fat
16 grams saturated fat
99 milligrams cholesterol
1 gram fiber
24 grams protein
316 milligrams sodium

STUFFED FLOUNDER FLORENTINE, PAGE 191

Each serving:
288 calories
18 grams carbohydrate
8 grams fat
2 grams saturated fat
83 milligrams cholesterol
6 grams fiber
34 grams protein
751 milligrams sodium

MAMMA ANTONIA'S AMAZING ALMOND COOKIES, PAGE 195

[2 cookies per serving]
Each serving:
133 calories
19 grams carbohydrate
6 grams fat
2 grams saturated fat
0 milligrams cholesterol
1 gram fiber
3 grams protein
34 milligrams sodium

LEMONITA GRANITA, PAGE 196

Each serving:
258 calories
68 grams carbohydrate
0 grams fat
0 grams saturated fat
0 milligrams cholesterol
0 grams fiber
0 grams protein
1 milligram sodium

BEAUTIFUL BISCOTTI, PAGE 199

[2 biscotti per serving]
Each serving:
174 calories
33 grams carbohydrate
3 grams fat
0 grams saturated fat
42 milligrams cholesterol
1 gram fiber
4 grams protein
53 milligrams sodium

CINNAMON HAZELNUT BISCOTTI, PAGE 200

[2 biscotti per serving]
Each serving:
198 calories
34 grams carbohydrate
5 grams fat
1 gram saturated fat
42 milligrams cholesterol
1 gram fiber
4 grams protein
53 milligrams sodium

ALMOND-ORANGE BISCOTTI, PAGE 200

[2 biscotti per serving]
Each serving:
175 calories
33 grams carbohydrate
3 grams fat
0 grams saturated fat
42 milligrams cholesterol
1 gram fiber
4 grams protein
53 milligrams sodium

DOUBLE CHOCOLATE BISCOTTI, PAGE 200

[2 biscotti per serving]
Each serving:
224 calories
39 grams carbohydrate
7 grams fat
3 grams saturated fat
42 milligrams cholesterol
2 grams fiber

5 grams protein
55 milligrams sodium

Chapter 11: ITALIAN DRESSING AND DELICIOUS SHOES

FENNEL SALAD, PAGE 214

Each serving:
83 calories
5 grams carbohydrate
7 grams fat
1 gram saturated fat
0 milligrams cholesterol
2 grams fiber
1 gram protein
177 milligrams sodium

PANZANELLA SALAD, PAGE 214

Each serving:
341 calories
28 grams carbohydrate
23 grams fat
4 grams saturated fat
5 milligrams cholesterol
2 grams fiber
7 grams protein
498 milligrams sodium

GIARDINO MINESTRONE, PAGE 216

Each serving:
113 calories
15 grams carbohydrate
4 grams fat
1 gram saturated fat
3 milligrams cholesterol
3 grams fiber
5 grams protein
257 milligrams sodium

PASTA UMBRIA, PAGE 217

Each serving:
473 calories
63 grams carbohydrate
19 grams fat
4 grams saturated fat

11 milligrams cholesterol
5 grams fiber
14 grams protein
296 milligrams sodium

SKINNY SNAPPER, PAGE 219

Each serving:
226 calories
9 grams carbohydrate
8 grams fat
1 gram saturated fat
50 milligrams cholesterol
3 grams fiber
30 grams protein
504 milligrams sodium

Chapter 12: LOVE-LOVE-LOVE

SPAGHETTI ALL'UBRIACO (DRUNKEN SPAGHETTI), PAGE 224

Each serving:
462 calories
70 grams carbohydrate
9 grams fat
2 grams saturated fat
6 milligrams cholesterol
6 grams fiber
16 grams protein
481 milligrams sodium

SICILIAN STEAK, PAGE 225

Each serving:
490 calories
7 grams carbohydrate
29 grams fat
10 grams saturated fat
112 milligrams cholesterol
1 gram fiber
47 grams protein
343 milligrams sodium

LUSCIOUS LINGUINE WITH MANILA CLAMS, PAGE 228

Each serving:
486 calories
59 grams carbohydrate

18 grams fat
5 grams saturated fat
29 milligrams cholesterol
2 grams fiber
18 grams protein
85 milligrams sodium

FRESH FRUIT WITH BEAUTIFUL BALSAMIC GLAZE, PAGE 231

Each serving:
90 calories
22 grams carbohydrate
0 grams fat
0 grams saturated fat
0 milligrams cholesterol
3 grams fiber
1 gram protein
6 milligrams sodium

FRESH STRAWBERRIES AND SAMBUCA, PAGE 232

Each serving:
151 calories
25 grams carbohydrate
0 grams fat
0 grams saturated fat
0 milligrams cholesterol
3 grams fiber
1 gram protein
2 milligrams sodium

PIZZA NUTELLA, PAGE 232

Each serving:
143 calories
20 grams carbohydrate
6 grams fat
1 gram saturated fat
0 milligrams cholesterol
1 gram fiber
3 grams protein
101 milligrams sodium

Index